A YEAR OF ZEN MINDFULNESS

ZEN MINDFULNESS

DAILY PRACTICES AND MEDITATIONS
TO FIND FOCUS AND PEACE

ALEX KAKUYO

ROCKRIDGE PRESS

For general information on our other products and services, please contact our Customer Care Department within the United States at (866) 744-2665, or outside the United States at (510) 253-0500.

Paperback ISBN: 978-1-63878-482-1
eBook ISBN: 978-1-63878-657-3

Manufactured in the United States of America

Interior and Cover Designer: Sean Doyle
Art Producer: Sara Feinstein
Editor: Carolyn Abate
Production Manager: Jose Olivera

Illustrations used under license from iStock.com.

10 9 8 7 6 5 4 3 2 1

THIS BOOK IS DEDICATED TO SUJATA.
Two thousand six hundred years ago she saw a hungry man dying in a river. She pulled him to safety and fed him rice milk. She saved his life. That man was the Buddha. Sujata changed the world with one act of kindness. May all beings learn from her example.

Contents

Introduction

Before I discovered meditation, I was living the American dream. I had a nice apartment on the "right" side of town. I drove my dream car, a green Ford Mustang, and I had a successful sales career that culminated in my winning an all-expenses paid trip to Cabo San Lucas, Mexico. On the surface, life was good. But I felt empty inside. And no amount of money, status, or material success could solve my problem.

In an act of desperation, I visited a Zen Buddhist temple, and something clicked. I found the path and the tools I needed to live a calmer, more peaceful life.

In the beginning, I had misconceptions about what "real" Zen entailed. I thought it required robes, painful sitting postures, and long retreats. In truth, I didn't know if I could practice Zen and still have a life that included a job, vacations, and spending time with family.

The author Robert M. Pirsig once said, "The only Zen you find on the tops of mountains is the Zen you bring up there." After many years of training, I can assure you that he was correct. I've carried my Zen with me all over the world. It accompanied me while I cared for chickens on a farm in upstate New York. It kept me warm during the winter when I built a tiny house in Indiana. And it helped me stay calm during meetings in corporate America.

Whether you are a devout Buddhist practitioner or someone with just a passing interest in mindfulness, it's my hope that this book will help you integrate spiritual practice with your daily life. We don't need to be monastics to walk the path. We just need to walk.

BASICS OF ZEN

Zen is a Japanese term that traces its roots to the Sanskrit word *dhyana*, meaning meditation or concentration. Often, when people think of Zen practice, they think of meditative practice, centered around single-pointed concentration. This can involve the seated meditation that you might associate with a Buddhist temple, but Zen is much more than that.

It's a lifestyle, a way of seeing the world that helps us eliminate distractions and live fully in this present moment. If done correctly, washing the dishes, cutting the grass, lying in bed, and, in fact, every facet of our life can embody Zen. That said, consistent practice is an important part of the training. It's better to do a little bit every day than to do a lot every once in a while.

This book contains affirmations, meditations, practices, writing prompts, and Zen koans to help you in your journey. Some of them will make you see the world in a different light, others will build your powers of concentration, and all of them will show you how to integrate a Zen way of thinking into your life.

Here are some notes on each of these elements:

- Affirmations: These are simple sayings that you can repeat throughout the day to create a positive mindset.

- Koans: A koan is a question that a teacher might ask a student to help them break out of dualistic thinking. In some sections, I pose a question with the expectation that you'll find the answer. In others, I give you the answer in the hopes that you'll find the question.

- Meditations: These are practices of single-pointed concentration that will make you less reactive to your thoughts.

- Practices: These mindfulness training exercises will help you experience the world in new and creative ways.

- Prompts: These are writing exercises that will help you break out of habitual thought patterns. Keep a journal or notebook handy, so you can complete them.

Some of this may seem strange or counterintuitive, but I encourage you to approach these teachings with an open mind. You're in charge of your practice. If something doesn't resonate with you, it's normal to "put it on the shelf" for a while and move on to the next exercise.

That said, I'm confident that this book will bring greater focus and more inner peace to your daily life.

JANUARY

1
JANUARY

—

Our mind decides if our life is good or bad. One person drinks a cup of tea and thinks it's delicious. Another person drinks from the same cup and thinks it's terrible. Who's right? What would happen if, instead of trying to change your life, you changed the way you thought about your life?

2
JANUARY

—

Roses have thorns, but we still love them. I don't need to be perfect to be loved.

3

Meditation:
BELLOWS BREATHING

Sit or lie down in a comfortable position in which you can breathe easily. Keep your back straight and your eyes open or closed. Breathe in and out through your nose, extending your belly button on each inhale like you just had a large meal. Relax on the exhale.

Focus on the physical sensations of breathing. Notice the feeling of your clothes against your skin. Feel the sensation of your belly expanding on every inhale and relaxing on every exhale.

If the mind starts to drift, gently notice your thoughts like you would notice birds flying through the sky. Mentally greet them and then bring your attention back to the physical sensation of breathing.

Repeat for 5 to 10 minutes.

4
JANUARY

Meditation:
MINDFUL WALKING OUTDOORS

Stand barefoot in a patch of grass. Breathe in and out through your nose. Continue breathing in this way and send your attention to the bottom of your feet. Notice the sensation of the grass against your skin. Flex your toes into the earth, noticing how that feels.

Let your intuition guide you. When it feels right, take a step with your left foot and recite this mantra out loud: "I am grounded. I am safe." Flex your toes into the earth, noticing how that feels. Rest in this moment for a while. When it feels like the time is right, take a step with your right foot and repeat the mantra: "I am grounded. I am safe."

If you are unable to stand or walk, sit on the grass and shift your head slowly from left to right. Breathe in concert with the movement of your head. Inhale when your head shifts to the left, and exhale when it shifts to the right.

Repeat for 5 to 10 minutes.

5
JANUARY

We're able to enjoy movies because we understand that they aren't real. If something bad happens on screen, we feel bad for a moment, but we don't hold on to those emotions. What would happen if you lived your life in the same way you watch movies?

6
JANUARY

Clouds float in the sky, but the sun is unbothered.
Thoughts float in my mind, but I am unbothered.

7

—

Meditation:
PLEASANT, UNPLEASANT, NEUTRAL

Sit or lie down in a comfortable position in which you can breathe easily. Keep your back straight and your eyes open or closed. Breathe in and out through your nose, extending your belly button on each inhale like you just had a large meal. Relax on the exhale.

Don't try to force yourself to think. But if thoughts do enter your mind, notice them on the inhale of each breath and label them on the exhale of each breath. Each thought can be pleasant, unpleasant, or neutral. It may be helpful to say the label out loud as part of the exhale.

Don't justify your responses or allow yourself to get pulled into stories. Just label the thought and return your focus to the breath.

Repeat for 5 to 10 minutes.

8

Meditation:
MINDFUL DROPS OF WATER

Fill a large bowl to the halfway point with lukewarm water. Place the bowl on a table and grab a small wash cloth. Put the wash cloth in the bowl and use your hand to push it to the bottom. Hold it there and notice the sensation of the water against your skin. Close your eyes and try to pinpoint the different sensations in the part of your arm that's under water compared with the part of your arm that's dry. Open your eyes and pull the wash cloth out of the bowl. Ring it out over the bowl and watch the water fall from it. Try to guess the exact moment when water will stop coming out of the cloth.

Repeat for 5 to 10 minutes.

9
JANUARY

If you have a pet, follow them around the house for five minutes. Write about what they do, noticing any feelings or memories that pop up. If you don't have a pet, observe animals at the local park or at a friend's house.

10
JANUARY

Many of life's problems would be solved if we thought of the planet as a house and everyone focused on being a good roommate.

11
JANUARY

—

It's okay to be scared. It's okay to be worried. Being emotional is not the same as being broken.

12
JANUARY

—

Meditation:
MINDFUL EATING

Sit down for a meal. Take a moment to offer gratitude to the people who made it possible. Name five colors that you see. How would you describe the food smells to someone who has never had this dish?

Poke at your food for a minute. Are there any interesting sounds or textures? Take a bite and examine how the food feels in your mouth. Swallow and don't move until you feel the food reach your stomach.

Repeat for 5 to 10 minutes.

13

Meditation:
LOVING THE INNER CHILD

Sit or lie down in a comfortable position in which you can breathe easily. Keep your back straight and your eyes open or closed. Breathe in and out through your nose, extending your belly button on each inhale like you just had a large meal. Relax on the exhale.

Find a picture of yourself as a child. Look at the picture and take a moment to connect with the younger version of you. Remember the likes, dislikes, and dreams you had at that age.

Smile at the picture of yourself and repeat these words aloud: "May you be happy. May you be healthy. May you be safe. May you be loved." Keep repeating the mantra slowly and gently.

Repeat for 5 to 10 minutes.

14
JANUARY

—

Set a timer for one minute and listen to the world around you. Write about the sounds you heard and how they made you feel.

15
JANUARY

—

Most of our life is spent doing ordinary, everyday things. But we want our life to be spent doing fun, exciting things. What would happen if you learned to have fun while doing ordinary, everyday things?

16
JANUARY

I've survived every bad thing that's happened to me.
I can handle any bad thing that happens today.

17
JANUARY

Toilets have an important job to do. They take the waste from our bodies and remove it so our homes don't become foul and smelly. Mindfulness is like a toilet for your mind.

18

Meditation:
TRACING CIRCLES

Sit or lie down in a comfortable position in which you can breathe easily. Keep your back straight and your eyes open or closed. Breathe in and out through your nose, extending your belly button on each inhale like you just had a large meal. Relax on the exhale.

Take a few moments to allow yourself to get centered in the breath. Place your hands palm down on either your thighs or your knees. Feel the sensation of your clothing beneath your fingertips.

On every inhale, use the index finger on your left hand to trace a circle on your left leg. On every exhale use the index finger on your right hand to trace a circle on your right leg. Continue breathing and tracing circles in this way.

Repeat for 5 to 10 minutes.

19

Meditation:
MINDFUL SLEEPING

Turn off all your devices and lie down in bed. Breathe in and out through your nose, extending your belly button on each inhale and relaxing on the exhale. Keep breathing in this way and listen to the sounds in the room. Give each one a one-word name like "fan" or "crickets."

Next, turn your palms downward and feel the sheets beneath your finger-tips. Are they smooth or rough? Are they hot or cold? Use your right hand to draw five circles with your fingers. When you're finished, do the same with your left hand.

Then bring your attention to your blankets. Are they heavy or light against your skin? Are they smooth or are they rough? Focus on the physical sensation of the blankets above you and the sheets below you. Keep breathing.

Repeat for 5 to 10 minutes.

20
JANUARY
—

What is your favorite time of the day? What are three things that you appreciate the most about it?

21
JANUARY
—

The little things make a big difference. Putting seeds in a bird feeder is a small thing, but it makes the birds happy. What are little things you do each day that bring joy to others?

22
JANUARY
—

The earth supports every step I take. I'm never alone because the earth is always with me.

23
JANUARY
—

How would you describe the ideal circumstances for mindfulness practice? Write down ways that you can recreate those circumstances in your daily life.

24
JANUARY

Meditation:
SPIRITUAL POWER

Sit or lie down in a comfortable position in which you can breathe easily. Keep your back straight and your eyes open or closed. Breathe in and out through your nose, extending your belly button on each inhale like you just had a large meal. Relax on the exhale.

Visualize a fire burning in your belly, in the space behind your belly button. Take a moment to notice the logs and hot coals at the bottom. Hear the crackling and sizzling of the wood as the flames leap into the air. This fire represents your spiritual power and you can call upon it whenever you need it.

With every inhale, feel the air entering your lungs. With every exhale, see yourself blowing on the base of the fire, feeding it oxygen, making it bigger and brighter with every breath.

Repeat for 5 to 10 minutes.

25

Meditation:
MINDFUL COOKING

Take out the ingredients and offer gratitude to the food for the nourishment you're about to receive. This can be done via a small nod of the head, a smile, or a slight bow. Note the color of each food that you will be preparing and the smell. Does this conjure any memories? Rub each one with your fingertips. Note the texture of each.

Think about what it was like to try these foods for the first time.
Repeat for 5 to 10 minutes.

26

JANUARY

Write about five beneficial things that you did for other people today. It can be as small as holding the door for someone.

27
JANUARY

Meditation:
PURIFYING THE CLOUD

Sit or lie down in a comfortable position in which you can breathe easily. Keep your back straight and your eyes open or closed. Breathe in and out through your nose, extending your belly button on each inhale like you just had a large meal. Relax on the exhale.

Visualize a ball of energy in the space behind your belly button. The energy ball is your favorite color. It gets a little bigger with every inhale and a little smaller with every exhale. Visualize a gray cloud surrounding your entire body.

The energy ball represents your spiritual power and the gray cloud represents your negative thoughts. With every inhale, breathe in a small piece of the cloud and send it down to the energy ball in your belly. When it gets there, the cloud piece is purified, changing to be the same color as the energy in your belly.

With every exhale, return the purified cloud piece to the gray cloud. Notice that as you continue breathing, the gray cloud of your negative thoughts slowly changes to be the same color as the energy ball in your belly.

Repeat for 5 to 10 minutes.

28

Meditation:
MINDFUL DISHWASHING

Stack the dirty dishes on the counter so that similar items are stacked together (plates on top of plates, bowls on top of bowls, etc.). Offer gratitude to the dishes for helping you eat your food. Take a moment to think about the meals you ate with them. Was the food good? Did other people eat with you? Begin placing the dishes in the sink and try to remember where each one came from. Did you buy it at the store, or was it a gift?

Wash a few of the dishes and place them in a drying rack. Notice how different they look now that they are clean. Is the process of washing dishes like the process of training our minds via mindfulness?

Repeat for 5 to 10 minutes.

29
JANUARY
———

Sometimes we suffer because we make things too complicated. Write about five commitments you can eliminate to simplify your life. Make plans to let them go. Some examples include taking on fewer projects at work or reducing social engagements.

30
JANUARY
———

In autumn, leaves fall from the trees. The trees don't suffer because they let them go. What are you holding on to that you should let go?

31
JANUARY

—

Meditation:
DIG INTO THE EARTH

Sit or lie down in a comfortable position in which you can breathe easily. Keep your back straight and your eyes open or closed. Breathe in and out through your nose, extending your belly button on each inhale like you just had a large meal. Relax on the exhale.

Position your palms so they're facing the ground. With every exhale, straighten your fingers. Visualize your arms growing longer, pushing your hands into the earth. Feel the texture of the dirt on your palms. With every inhale, contract your fingers slightly and visualize your hands grabbing hold of the dirt, anchoring your body in place.

Repeat for 5 to 10 minutes.

FEBRUARY

1
FEBRUARY

Cats live simple lives. Once they have food, water, and a safe place to sleep, they are satisfied. People live complicated lives; we always want more than we have. What would happen if you followed the example of cats?

2
FEBRUARY

I can control my breath. I cannot control the world. If everything spins into chaos, I'll focus on controlling my breath.

3

Meditation:
VOLCANO BREATHING

Sit or lie down in a comfortable position in which you can breathe easily. Keep your back straight and your eyes open or closed. Breathe in and out through your nose, extending your belly button on each inhale like you just had a large meal. Relax on the exhale.

Visualize a hollow sphere forming in the space behind your belly button. The sphere has one pipe that goes down to the center of Earth. It has a second pipe that goes up to the top of your head.

With every inhale, visualize yourself pulling hot magma up from the center of Earth and storing it in the empty space in your belly. With every exhale, see that magma going up the pipe toward the top of your head until it explodes outward like a volcano, showering your body in warm, healing light.

Repeat for 5 to 10 minutes.

4

Meditation:
MINDFUL PICTURE-TAKING INDOORS

Open the camera app on your phone. Look around the room. Pick a piece of furniture that you want to use for the picture. Take a few moments and think about your relationship with the object. Has it been in your life a long time? How did it get in the room?

Take a few pictures of the object from different angles. Look at the pictures and notice any shadows or strange effects that are coming from the light in the room.

Pick a specific characteristic of the object that you find interesting and get close to it with your camera. Take several pictures of it from different angles. Look at the close-up pictures. Are there any details that you notice when getting close-up that you couldn't see from farther away? How is this a metaphor for life?

Repeat for 5 to 10 minutes.

5
FEBRUARY

—

Spend an hour on social media, then turn off all your devices, and write down the thoughts/feelings that you experienced.

6
FEBRUARY

—

For a houseplant to thrive, they must have healthy soil. Your mind is a houseplant and your daily activities are the soil. Are you creating soil that helps or hurts your mind?

7
FEBRUARY

I am alive. I am alert. I can respond skillfully
to anything that happens to me.

8
FEBRUARY

Meditation:
COUNTING BREATHS

Sit or lie down in a comfortable position in which you can breathe easily. Keep your back straight. Breathe in and out through your nose, extending your belly button on each inhale. Relax on the exhale.

On the first exhale, count "one" either aloud or in your head. On the second exhale, count "two." Keep counting your breaths until you get to ten and then start over at one. If the mind wanders, notice your thoughts, and gently bring your focus back. Repeat for 5 to 10 minutes.

9

What's your favorite place in the world?
How would you describe it to someone who
has only seen the inside of a dark cave?
Hint: Use all your senses to explain it.

10

Meditation:
MINDFUL WALKING INDOORS

Stand barefoot on the floor. Breathe in and out through your nose. Continue breathing in this way and send your attention to the bottom of your feet. Notice the sensation of the floor against your skin. Stand on tiptoe for a moment and notice the shifting of weight on the soles of your feet. If standing is uncomfortable for you, you can also do this by sitting in a chair and moving your feet.

Let your intuition guide you. When it feels right, move your left foot, pause for a moment, and then bring your right foot even with your left. Stand on tiptoe for a moment and notice the shifting of weight on the bottom of your feet.

When it feels appropriate, move your right foot, pause for a moment, and then bring your left foot even with your right. Stand on tiptoe for a moment and notice the shifting of weight on the bottom of your feet. Continue alternating in this way until you reach the end of the room (or, if seated, after a certain count).

Repeat for 5 to 10 minutes.

11
FEBRUARY

Look around the room. Write down five items that are blue, five items that are red, and five items that are green.

12
FEBRUARY

A daily commute can be a source of suffering. But if it's something you must do, how can we make it more enjoyable?

13
FEBRUARY

———

I possess inner wisdom that is pure and undefiled. I can trust my intuition to help me make good decisions.

14
FEBRUARY

———

Meditation:
MINDFUL CLOUD GAZING

Lie down in the grass. Breathe in and out through your nose with your arms next to you, palms facing up. Observe your limbs and feel them press into the ground.

Look up at the sky and count the clouds you see without moving your head. Feel your body sinking deeper into the ground with each breath. How does it feel to allow things to come to you instead of chasing them?

Repeat for 5 to 10 minutes.

15
FEBRUARY

Eat a meal. Pay close attention to the
temperature, taste, and texture of the food as
you chew it. Write down your experience.

16
FEBRUARY

Many people dislike washing dishes, but it's something we must do.
Instead of being upset over dirty dishes, can you be grateful that
you have dishes to eat from?

17
FEBRUARY

—

I'm a piece of bamboo. I grow stronger every day. In the face of adversity I bend, but I don't break.

18
FEBRUARY

—

Meditation:
MINDFUL SWEEPING

Pick up a broom and stand in a corner of the room. Offer gratitude to the broom for helping you clean. Hold the broom so that it's parallel to the floor with your palms facing the ceiling. Notice the weight of it in your hands. Notice its color and texture.

Look over the room you're about to clean. What have you done in there today? Are there parts of the floor that are dirtier than others?

As you sweep the room, observe the sound of the broom on the floor.

19

Who is your favorite music artist? Listen to three of their songs and write down your experience. What memories pop up? What happens in your body?

20

When our hands are cold, we put them in our pockets. We care for them without thinking because they are a part of us. What would happen if you treated other people as if they were your hands?

21
FEBRUARY

Meditation:
MINDFUL COFFEE-MAKING

Hold a package of ground coffee beans in your hand and notice the texture. Squeeze it a few times. What are your impressions of the beans inside, based on what you feel? Offer gratitude to the farmers who harvested those beans.

Open the package of coffee and smell the beans. Do they bring up any memories? Is it a pleasant aroma? Look closely at the beans and notice if they are black or brown. Shake the package around a bit and watch how they shift.

Measure out the amount of coffee beans you prefer and pour them into the coffee filter. Notice the patterns made by the beans as they fall into the filter. Take a moment to notice how much the package of coffee beans has been depleted, then close the bag. Notice the change of weight in the bag.

Turn on the coffee maker and listen to the sound of the coffee as it drips into the bottom of the pot.

Repeat for 5 to 10 minutes.

22

Meditation:
MINDFUL STARGAZING

Lie down in the grass on a starry night. Place your arms on either side of your body, palms up. Breathe in and out through your nose. Continue breathing in this way and send your attention to the back of your head and shoulders. Take a moment and feel them sinking into the ground. Next, direct your attention to your legs and the heels of your feet. Gently press them into the earth.

Look up at the sky and count how many stars you see without moving your head. Feel your body sinking deeper into the ground and hold this position for five breaths.

Shift your vision slightly to the left. Notice how different the sky looks with this slight shift in viewpoint. Is this a metaphor for life?

Hold your head in this position for five breaths and then shift your vision back to center. Close your eyes and try to remember what the sky looks like. Do this for 10 breaths, then open your eyes.

Repeat for 5 to 10 minutes.

23
FEBRUARY
—

Write down something that you've been trying to fix for a long time, but remains broken. Would your life improve if you stopped trying to fix it?

24
FEBRUARY
—

Meditation:
MINDFUL BELLY RUBS

Sit or lie down in a comfortable position in which you can breathe easily. Keep your back straight. Breathe deeply through your nose with your right hand on your chest to observe your heartbeat and your left hand on your belly. Do this for five breaths and switch hand positions without breaking contact between your hands and body. Hold this position for five breaths and then switch hands. Repeat for 5 to 10 minutes.

25
FEBRUARY

—

What are five things that you do every day solely to make other people happy? Write down how your life would change if you stopped doing them.

26
FEBRUARY

—

Meditation:
MINDFUL BREATHING—WITH A PET PARTNER

Breathe deeply through your nose. While breathing, observe your pet and offer them gratitude.

Pay close attention to the rise and fall of their belly. Change your breathing so that it's in sync with theirs.

If you don't have a pet, watch a video of an animal.

Repeat for 5 to 10 minutes.

27
FEBRUARY

What is your favorite time of year? How would you describe it to a space alien who has never been to Earth?

28
FEBRUARY

Take a moment to contemplate the sun and the moon. What are their qualities? Which one do you resonate with the most?

MARCH

1
MARCH

It's hard work to care for a garden, but the basic idea is simple. Plant the seeds of what you want to grow and pull out all the weeds. Our minds function like gardens. What kind of seeds are you planting in your mind? How are you planting those seeds?

2
MARCH

The moon changes throughout the month, but it is always beautiful. My mind changes throughout the day, but it is always beautiful.

3
MARCH

Meditation:
NOTICING PHYSICAL SENSATIONS

Sit or lie down in a comfortable position in which you can breathe easily. Keep your back straight and your eyes open or closed. Breathe in and out through your nose, extending your belly button on each inhale like you just had a large meal. Relax on the exhale.

Direct your focus to your feet. Notice the physical sensations in your feet without judgment. Pay attention to the feeling of the floor, the weight of your socks/shoes against your skin. Are your feet hot or cold? Stay with your feet for five breaths and then shift your focus to your legs. Next, do your torso, then your arms, and finally your head.

After you finish with your head, return your focus to your feet.

Repeat for 5 to 10 minutes.

4
MARCH

—

Meditation:
MINDFUL MOPPING

Pick up the mop and position yourself in a corner of the room you want to clean. Offer gratitude to the mop for helping you clean. Hold the mop so that it's parallel to the floor with your palms facing the ceiling. Notice the weight of it in your hands. Notice the color and texture of the handle. Is it made from wood or plastic?

Look over the room you're about to clean. What have you done there today? Are there parts of the floor that are dirtier than others?

Put the mop in a bucket of water and pull it out. Listen to the sound of water falling back into the bucket. Reach down with one hand and wring out the mop. Pay attention to the contrasting sensations of water and the mop strands against your skin.

Repeat for 5 to 10 minutes.

5
MARCH

What are the most important things you look for in a friend or romantic partner? How can you give those things to yourself?

6
MARCH

A campfire is both beautiful and dangerous. If we get too close, it will burn us. If we move too far away, we'll be cold. But if we practice the middle-way between these extremes, we can be warm, cook food, and enjoy time around the fire with friends. What would happen if you practiced the middle-way with everything in life?

7
MARCH

—

I can find everything I need in this present
moment. If I can't find it here, I don't need it.

8
MARCH

What is your favorite color? How would
you describe it to a space alien who
lives on a planet with no colors? Use
your other four senses as a guide.

9
MARCH

Meditation:
SELF-LOVE MANTRAS

Sit or lie down in a comfortable position in which you can breathe easily. Keep your back straight and your eyes open or closed. Breathe in and out through your nose, extending your belly button on each inhale like you just had a large meal. Relax on the exhale.

Once you have settled into your breath, inhale. With the first exhale, say, "I am happy." Inhale, and with the second exhale, say, "I am healthy." Inhale, and with the third exhale say, "I am loved." Continue breathing and reciting the mantras in this way.

Repeat for 5 to 10 minutes.

10
MARCH

Meditation:
MINDFUL TYPING

Look down at the keyboard. Offer gratitude to the keys for helping you get your ideas into the world. Notice the colors and shapes of the keys. Does the keyboard have any stickers on it? Rest your fingertips on the keyboard. Is it warm or cold? What is the texture of the board?

Begin typing and listen to the sound of the keys tapping. Do some letters sound different from others?

Repeat for 5 to 10 minutes.

11
MARCH

If you had to live in the woods, the mountains, or on the beach for the rest of your life, which would you pick? How would you spend your days?

12
MARCH

If a window is dirty, we clean it so sunlight can enter the house. If our mind is dirty, we clean it (with mindfulness) so sunlight can enter our life.

13
MARCH

I deserve rest. I deserve compassion. I can say no to obligations to give myself rest and compassion.

14
MARCH

—

Meditation:
HEALING HANDS

Sit or lie down in a comfortable position in which you can breathe easily. Keep your back straight and your eyes open or closed. Breathe in and out through your nose, extending your belly button on each inhale like you just had a large meal. Relax on the exhale.

Place your palms together in front of your chest. Rub your hands together briskly for five breaths. Direct healing energy to your hands as you do this.

Next, place your right hand over your heart and your left hand over your belly button. Direct healing energy into your heart and belly. Remain in this position for 10 breaths. After that, continue alternating between rubbing your hands together and placing them on your body.

Repeat for 5 to 10 minutes.

15

—

Meditation:
MINDFUL CONVERSATION

Look at the person who is speaking to you. Offer them gratitude for connecting with you in this way. Look them in the eye. Listen to their tone of voice. Do they sound calm, excited, or scared? Pay close attention and see if you can catch the last word of their sentences. During lulls in the conversation, make sure you are understanding clearly by saying, "It sounds like what you are saying is _____," and then repeat back what you heard.

Repeat for 5 to 10 minutes.

16
MARCH

—

Sit for five minutes with your eyes closed. Experience the world using your other senses and write down what you notice.

17
MARCH
———

An ordinary person takes pleasure in their own accomplishments. An extraordinary person takes pleasure in the accomplishments of others.

18
MARCH
———

I'm at my best in difficult situations. I breathe in negativity and breathe out love, healing the world with every breath.

19
MARCH

Meditation:
LOVING YOUR INNER TEENAGER

Sit or lie down in a comfortable position in which you can breathe easily. Keep your back straight and your eyes open or closed. Breathe in and out through your nose, extending your belly button on each inhale like you just had a large meal. Relax on the exhale.

Look at a picture of yourself as a teenager. Take a moment to connect with the younger version of you. Remember your likes, your dislikes, and your dreams for the future.

Smile at the picture of yourself as a teenager and repeat these words aloud: "May you be happy. May you be healthy. May you be safe. May you be loved." Keep repeating the mantra slowly and gently.

Repeat for 5 to 10 minutes.

20
MARCH

—

Meditation:
MINDFUL SOCIAL MEDIA

Before you log in, ask yourself, "Why am I visiting this site?" Is there information that you want to obtain? Do you need to send a message to a relative or a friend? Think back to the last time you were on the site, and if it's likely that anything noteworthy has happened between then and now. If not, are there better ways to spend your time?

Pay attention to your emotional state when you log in. Are you happy, fearful, sad? Notice the other people who are posting. What are the ideas/emotions that they're conveying? Do they feel healthy and life-affirming?

Scroll through the site and make a few posts. Check in with yourself again to see how you are feeling. What memories are popping up because of this experience. Are they happy ones?

Repeat for 5 to 10 minutes.

21
MARCH

What is your favorite food? How would you describe it to someone who has no sense of taste?

22
MARCH

We cannot choose our thoughts. We cannot choose our emotions. But we can choose how we respond to our thoughts and our emotions.

23
MARCH

My spiritual power burns like a fire in my belly. I can call on it whenever I need to.

24
MARCH

Meditation:
OPEN AND CLOSE

Sit or lie down in a comfortable position in which you can breathe easily. Keep your back straight. Breathe in and out through your nose, extending your belly button on each inhale like you just had a large meal. Relax on the exhale.

Place your hands on either side of your body, palms up. On every inhale, flex your hands open. With every exhale, close them into light fists. Notice the physical sensations of your fingers moving and touching your skin.

Repeat for 5 to 10 minutes.

25
MARCH

—

Meditation:
MINDFUL NEWS STORIES

Before you check the news, ask yourself "Why am I doing this?" Is there information that you want to obtain? Think back to the last time you checked the news,
and if it's likely that anything noteworthy has happened between then and now.
If not, are there better ways to spend your time?

When you turn on the news, pay attention to your emotional state. Are
you happy, fearful, or sad? Who are you getting your reporting from? Do they
normally leave you in a calm, uplifted state, or do their reports make you feel
cynical and angry?

Is your mental state better when you get news from a newspaper, a TV pro-
gram, or some other source?

Repeat for 5 to 10 minutes.

26
MARCH

——

Think about where you want to be in three years. Write down five things you need to accomplish to get there. Decide if getting what you want is worth the effort.

27
MARCH

——

The teacher asked, "What is the sound of one hand clapping?" The student responded by giving him a high five.

28
MARCH

Meditation:
GROWING A ROSE

Sit or lie down in a comfortable position in which you can breathe easily. Keep your back straight and your eyes open or closed. Breathe in and out through your nose, extending your belly button on each inhale like you just had a large meal. Relax on the exhale.

Visualize a clay pot in front of you that's filled with soil. See yourself planting a single rose seed into the soil. With every breath, send loving energy to the seed. Watch the roots slowly form and spread out in the soil as a tiny green stem moves toward the surface. Visualize the stem breaking the surface of the soil and sprouting leaves.

Continue sending loving energy to the rose as it grows to about six inches in height and a flower begins to open at its top. Watch as the rose blooms. Notice the silky nature of the flower petals. See if you can smell it.

Repeat for 5 to 10 minutes.

29
MARCH

Describe your life in one word. Let that one word ruminate in your mind for a while and write about the feelings that come up.

30
MARCH

Roses have thorns, but that doesn't stop them from being beautiful. Trees have crooked trunks, but that doesn't stop them from providing shade.

31
MARCH

—

Meditation:
LOVE KNOCKS

Sit or lie down on the floor in a comfortable position in which you can breathe easily. Keep your back straight and your eyes open or closed. Breathe in and out through your nose, extending your belly button on each inhale like you just had a large meal. Relax on the exhale.

Ball your hands up lightly into fists. Place them on either side of your body so your knuckles are touching the floor. On every inhale, knock once on the floor with your right fist, just like you would if you were knocking on a door. On every exhale, knock twice on the floor with your left fist.

Focus your attention on the sound of your fists connecting with the floor. Repeat for 5 to 10 minutes.

APRIL

1
APRIL

If a mirror is broken, we replace it. What would happen if you replaced all the broken things in your life?

2
APRIL

The universe doesn't make mistakes. I'm here because I'm supposed to be here, doing exactly what I'm doing in this moment.

3
APRIL

—

Meditation:
STAND LIKE A TREE

Sit or lie down in a comfortable position in which you can breathe easily. Keep your back straight and your eyes open or closed. Breathe in and out through your nose, extending your belly button on each inhale like you just had a large meal. Relax on the exhale.

Visualize yourself standing in an open field. Watch your feet transform into tree roots. They are hard and woody as they sink down into the soil. See your skin transform into bark, as your arm hairs become tree branches. Each of your branches sprout bright green leaves. You are a tree.

Rest in the feeling of being a tree for a while, then notice your thoughts. They are wind moving through your branches. Sometimes the wind is strong, sometimes it is weak. But your roots run deep and you are unbothered. Just sway gently with them and let them pass.

Repeat for 5 to 10 minutes.

4
APRIL

—

Meditation:

MINDFUL BREATHING—WITH HUMAN PARTNER

Sit cross-legged across from a partner or lie down next to them. If you lie down, position yourself so you can see the front of their body clearly. Breathe in and out through your nose, extending your belly button on every inhale and relaxing on every exhale. Place your right hand over your heart, and place your left hand over your belly button. Notice the feeling of your belly expanding and contracting.

Ask your partner to do the same. Once both of you are breathing in this manner, try to synch up your breathing by watching your partner's hand move up and down on their belly.

If you live alone or don't have an available partner, practice mindful breathing on your own. Focus on the feeling of air moving up and down your throat. Notice the expansion and contraction of your belly.

Repeat for 5 to 10 minutes.

5
APRIL

What does loyalty mean to you? Who are the most loyal people in your life and how do you know that they are loyal?

6
APRIL

A child was playing next to a river. He slammed a stick into the water to see what would happen. The river responded by continuing its journey to the ocean.

7
APRIL

My mind is not separate from my body. I can train my body to be strong. I can train my mind to be strong.

8
APRIL

When summer turns to fall, trees drop their leaves without complaint. When life becomes difficult, I drop my expectations without complaint.

9
APRIL

—

Meditation:
SIT WITH A TREE

Sit or lie down next to a tree in a comfortable position in which you can breathe easily. Keep your back straight and your eyes open or closed. Breathe in and out through your nose, extending your belly button on each inhale like you just had a large meal. Relax on the exhale.

Place your palms against the bark of the tree. Visualize a green aura surrounding the tree: this represents the tree's power of purification. See a blue ball of energy in the space behind your forehead: this represents your thoughts.

With every exhale, visualize yourself sending your thoughts from your head, through your arms into the purifying aura of the tree. With every inhale, see the purified thoughts coming back from the tree, filling your mind with positive energy.

Repeat for 5 to 10 minutes.

10
APRIL

—

Meditation:
MINDFUL JUMPING

Stand with your feet shoulder-width apart and your knees slightly bent. Place your right hand over your heart and your left hand over your belly. Offer gratitude to your heart for keeping you alive and try to feel it beating through your chest. Breathe in and out through your nose, extending your belly button on the inhale and relaxing on the exhale. Do this for five breaths.

Drop your hands so they hang loosely at your sides and jump up and down as high as you can 10 times. Pay attention to the physical sensations in the bottom of your feet as your jump.

After the tenth jump, place your right hand over your heart and your left hand over your belly. Feel your elevated heart rate and resume breathing through your nose. Stay in this position until your heart rate returns to normal, then do 10 more jumps.

If you are unable to stand or walk, shift your head slowly from left to right. And breathe in concert with the movement of your head. Inhale when your head shifts to the left, exhale when it shifts to the right.

Repeat for 5 to 10 minutes.

11
APRIL
___

If your life was a movie, would you be the hero or the villain? Thinking of your life as a movie can provide distance and give a clearer picture of how you relate to others.

12
APRIL
___

Every time we build a sandcastle on the beach, the ocean washes it away. But it's still fun to build sandcastles.

13
APRIL

—

Meditation:
RESTING ON THE BEACH

Sit or lie down in a comfortable position in which you can breathe easily. Keep your back straight and your eyes open or closed. Breathe in and out through your nose, extending your belly button on each inhale like you just had a large meal. Relax on the exhale.

See yourself sitting on a beach. Visualize the ocean waves crashing against the sand. See the sunlight glimmering on the water and feel the coarse sand rubbing against your legs. As you sit, visualize your thoughts popping up all over the beach in the form of small sandcastles. With every inhale, see the waves washing over the sandcastle-thoughts. And with every exhale, watch the waves go back into the ocean, leaving nothing behind.

Rest in the moment between when the waves wash your sandcastle-thoughts away and when new ones pop up.

Repeat for 5 to 10 minutes.

14
APRIL

Meditation:
MINDFUL CEREAL

Pour yourself a bowl of cereal and sit down at a table to eat. Look down at the bowl and try to remember the first time you had this brand of cereal. Who were you with? Did you enjoy the meal? Bend over and get a good look at the cereal. Do you notice any interesting colors or textures? Take a whiff of the cereal. What does it smell like? Use your spoon to take a bite of the cereal, noticing the flavor sensations on your tongue.

15
APRIL

What are the emotional states that you value the most? Write down five things in your life that cause you to feel them.

16
APRIL
—

If we help a single tree flourish, we provide shelter, shade, and food for countless animals. How much good could you do if you helped a single person flourish?

17
APRIL
—

I am smart. I am capable. I have all the tools I need to succeed.

18
APRIL

—

Meditation:
MINDFUL LEAF GAZING

Sit or stand over a pile of leaves. Look at them and see if you notice any patterns. Pick up one of the leaves and give it a big whiff. How would you describe the smell? Rub the leaf between the palms of your hands. Is it dry and crumbly or wet and slimy? Hold the leaf parallel to the ground and then at eye level. Notice any lines, colors, and patterns that you couldn't see when it was on the ground. Drop the leaf and watch it until it hits the ground.

Repeat for 5 to 10 minutes.

19
APRIL

—

What are the emotional states that you dread? Write down five things in your life that cause you to feel them.

20
APRIL

The darkness of a cocoon is required for a caterpillar to grow wings.

21
APRIL

My true nature is wise and compassionate.
When I walk out my front door, my wisdom and
compassion improve the world around me.

22
APRIL

___

Meditation:
MINDFUL COLORS

Move around your home and find five things that are blue; touch them with your hands. Find five things that are red; smell them with your nose. Find five things that are orange; shake them to see if they make a sound. Find five foods that are green; take a bite to see how they taste. Find five things that are yellow; pick them up and look at them closely.

23
APRIL

___

What are the emotional states that you experience most often? Write down five things in your life that cause you to feel them.

24
APRIL
—

A fire doesn't burn by itself. It requires fuel and a spark. What is the fuel for your fire and have you found your spark?

25
APRIL
—

What is your favorite hobby? If you could go back in time, what would you tell yourself on the first day you discovered it?

26
APRIL

———

If you always carry an umbrella, you never have to worry about the rain.

27
APRIL

———

What are your favorite things about yourself?

28
APRIL

Life is filled with cloudy days, but the sun always comes out eventually. Sometimes, the best response to hardship is patience.

29
APRIL

Write down your usual strategies for responding to hardship. Are they helpful? If not, what are some new strategies that you can replace them with?

30
APRIL

When dogs are playing, they only think about playing. When dogs are sleeping, they only think about sleep. That's why dogs are happier than people.

MAY

1
MAY

If we cherish something, it's not uncommon to build a fence around it to keep it safe. Setting healthy boundaries and enforcing them is one way to cherish ourselves.

2
MAY

I approach life with a mindset of abundance. I enjoy sharing my knowledge and skills with others.

3
MAY

Meditation:
WINDBLOWN SAND

Sit or lie down in a comfortable position in which you can breathe easily. Keep your back straight. Breathe in and out through your nose, extending your belly button on each inhale like you just had a large meal. Relax on the exhale.

See yourself sitting on a beach. Visualize the ocean waves crashing against the sand. See the sunlight glimmering on the water and feel the coarse sand rubbing against your legs. As you sit, visualize yourself scooping sand into the palms of your hands. Hold it at eye level and study the individual grains of sand.

As thoughts come into your head, channel them into the handfuls of sand. Then watch as a gentle wind blows the sand and your thoughts away. Each time new thoughts come into your head, scoop up another handful of sand.

Try to rest in the moment between when the wind blows your sand-thoughts away and when you scoop up another handful.

Repeat for 5 to 10 minutes.

4
MAY

Meditation:
MINDFUL TEXTURES

Move around your home and find five items that have a rough texture. Find five items that have a smooth texture. Find five items that have a bumpy texture. Find five items that are clean. Find five items that are dirty.

Repeat for 5 to 10 minutes.

5
MAY

Write a letter to your bank account. Discuss your relationship and whether you think it's healthy.

6
MAY

When we make the decision to express gratitude, we find reasons to be grateful. When we make the decision to express resentment, we find reasons to be resentful.

7
MAY

My mindfulness practice helps me stay focused amid distractions. I stick with tasks until they're completed to my satisfaction.

8

Meditation:
FLOAT TOWARD THE SUN

Sit or lie down in a comfortable position in which you can breathe easily. Keep your back straight and your eyes open or closed. Breathe in and out through your nose, extending your belly button on each inhale like you just had a large meal. Relax on the exhale.

Visualize yourself floating in the air, moving toward a beautiful sunset. Picture your thoughts as white fluffy clouds floating in the air around you. As the clouds come near you, label each one with a single word like "work" or "break-up" and then see yourself floating over them. Don't look back as they pass you by.

Repeat for 5 to 10 minutes.

9
MAY

Meditation:
MINDFUL "SHORT — SHORT — LONG" BREATHING

Sit in a comfortable position or lie down on the floor, belly up with your hands resting at your sides. Place your right hand over your heart and your left hand over your belly button. Breathe in through your nose in two short inhalations. Extend your belly as if you just had a large meal with each inhale. The goal is to fill your lungs with as much air as possible. On the exhale, relax your body and keep going until it feels like you've emptied your lungs without straining.

Repeat for 5 to 10 minutes.

10
MAY

Fill in the blank: When I feel angry, I _____.
Look at your answer and write about how
it makes you feel. Are you proud of it?

11
MAY

A Buddhist monk walked into a pizza shop and said, "Make me one with everything." The pizza shop owner replied by giving the monk an empty pizza box.

12
MAY

I am choosy about the obligations I take on. I trust my intuition to tell me when I should say yes to people and when I should say no.

13
MAY

Meditation:
FLY THROUGH THE FOREST

Sit or lie down in a comfortable position in which you can breathe easily. Keep your back straight and your eyes open or closed. Breathe in and out through your nose, extending your belly button on each inhale like you just had a large meal. Relax on the exhale.

Visualize yourself floating about three feet off the ground. You are in a forest, surrounded by pine trees. The ground is littered with pinecones and dead, brown pine needles. Take a whiff and see if you can smell the trees.

See yourself flying forward, picking up speed as you go. The pine trees represent your thoughts. Each time one pops up in front of you, label it with a single word like "sad" or "frustrated" and then fly past it. Don't look back.

Repeat for 5 to 10 minutes.

14
MAY

Meditation:
MINDFUL PUSHING AND PULLING OF AIR

Place your dominant hand in front of your face. Exhale through the nose, touching your fingertips to your thumb and moving your hand away in rhythm with your exhalation.

Open your hand so that's gently cupped. On your inhale, move it toward your face. Continue breathing in that way, envisioning yourself pulling air from your lungs with every exhale and pushing air into your lungs with every inhale.

Repeat for 5 to 10 minutes.

15
MAY

When I feel overwhelmed, I ____. How does your answer make you feel? Are there ways to improve?

16
MAY

A student sat down in front of their Buddhist teacher and said, "I'm so upset. My to-do list is a mile long, and I don't know if I can finish it all." The teacher responded by telling the student to write down everything on their to-do list. When the student finished, the teacher took the list, crumpled it up, and threw it into a trash can. "All done," the teacher said.

17
MAY

My time is valuable. I utilize the 24 hours of each day to ensure that I am well-rested, well-fed, and emotionally nourished.

18
MAY

—

Meditation:
HOT AIR BALLOON RIDE

Sit or lie down in a comfortable position in which you can breathe easily. Keep your back straight and your eyes open or closed. Breathe in and out through your nose, extending your belly button on each inhale like you just had a large meal. Relax on the exhale.

Visualize yourself riding in a hot air balloon. There is blue sky all around you, and when you look down you see lakes and snow-covered mountains. Reach down and feel the wicker basket beneath your fingertips.

With every inhale, the hot air balloon goes higher into the air. And with every exhale, it drops down toward the mountain. If your mind wanders, say "hello" to your thoughts and bring your focus back to your breathing and the visualization.

Repeat for 5 to 10 minutes.

19
MAY

MINDFUL BREATHING—WALKING BREATHS

Stand at the edge of a room with your back to the wall. Place your feet shoulder-width apart and let your hands hang toward the floor. Breathe in and out through your nose, extending your belly button on every inhale and relaxing on every exhale.

On every inhale, walk forward with slow, measured steps. On every exhale, stand still with your hands hanging loosely toward the floor. Notice the physical sensation of your breathing and the sensation of your feet touching the floor. When you reach the opposite side of the room, turn around and continue walking.

If you are unable to stand or walk, shift your head slowly from left to right. Breathe in concert with the movement of your head. Inhale when your head shifts to the left, and exhale when it shifts to the right. Notice the physical sensation of your breathing and your body touching the chair.

Repeat for 5 to 10 minutes.

20
MAY

Write down the five people you know you can go to in an emergency.

21
MAY

A student sat down in front of his teacher and complained, "There just isn't enough time in the day." The teacher replied, "Show me your time, and I'll give you more."

22
MAY

—

Meditation:
LEAF IN THE WIND

Sit or lie down in a comfortable position in which you can breathe easily. Keep your back straight and your eyes open or closed. Breathe in and out through your nose, extending your belly button on each inhale like you just had a large meal. Relax on the exhale.

Imagine yourself as a green leaf, floating on the wind. Above you, there is a blue sky with white fluffy clouds; below you, there is a meadow filled with flowers.

With every inhale, you float up toward the clouds. And with every exhale, you drop down toward the flowers. If your mind wanders, say "hello" to your thoughts and bring your focus back to your breathing and the visualization.

Repeat for 5 to 10 minutes.

23
MAY

What is your favorite childhood memory?
Write about that experience and try to
recall as many details as possible.

24
MAY

A student sat down in front of their teacher and said, "I don't know
what to do. There's a person who doesn't like me, and it ruins
my day every time I read their social media posts." The teacher
replied, "If their social media posts upset you, why do you keep
reading them?"

25
MAY

I study the lives and writings of people who are successful in my field. I use their wisdom to find success in my endeavors.

26
MAY

A student sat down in front of their teacher and asked, "What's the easiest way to save the world?" The teacher replied, "Be kind to your neighbor, be kind to yourself." The student asked, "How will that save the world?" The teacher replied, "What do you call the world?"

27
MAY

—

Meditation:

TOY CARS IN THE LIVING ROOM

Sit or lie down in a comfortable position in which you can breathe easily. Keep your back straight and your eyes open or closed. Breathe in and out through your nose, extending your belly button on each inhale like you just had a large meal. Relax on the exhale.

See yourself sitting in your living room. Look around for a moment and look at the furniture, the walls, and the pictures on the walls. Imagine the room in as much detail as possible.

Notice that your thoughts appear on the living room floor in the form of toy cars. Each time one pops up, label it as either pleasant, unpleasant, or neutral. With every exhale, visualize a small tornado moving across your living room floor, carrying away any thought-cars that are there.

Repeat for 5 to 10 minutes.

28
MAY

—

Meditation:
MINDFUL MIRROR CLEANING

Stand in front of a mirror with a paper towel and a bottle of glass cleaner. Offer gratitude to the mirror for the many times it helped you get ready for your day. Notice the places where the mirror is dirty and notice the places where it is clean. Spray the mirror with the glass cleaner. Starting at the top-left corner of the mirror, wipe the paper towel horizontally across it. Repeat this motion below where you just cleaned. Continue wiping the mirror and recite this mantra with each wipe: "As I clean the mirror, I clean my mind."

Repeat for 5 to 10 minutes.

29
MAY

If you were a tree, what kind of tree would you be, and what would your life be like?

30
MAY

—

Meditation:
TRACING CIRCLES IN YOUR PALM

Sit or lie down in a comfortable position in which you can breathe easily. Keep your back straight and your eyes open or closed. Breathe in and out through your nose, extending your belly button on each inhale like you just had a large meal. Relax on the exhale.

Place your left hand on your lap with your palm facing your chin. With your right hand, take your index finger and touch the palm of your left hand. With every inhale, use your index finger to trace small, clockwise circles in your left hand. With every exhale, use your index finger to trace small, counterclockwise circles in your left hand. Focus on the physical sensations in your palm and your finger.

Repeat for 5 to 10 minutes.

31
MAY

Move around the room and rub your hands over the walls, furniture, houseplants, etc. Write down five items that are rough, five that are smooth, and five that are in between.

JUNE

1
JUNE

A student sat down in front of their teacher and asked, "Why is the sky blue?" The teacher replied, "Because people like to call it that." The student said, "That can't be the only reason." The teacher asked, "Is the sky red?" "No," the student replied, "the sky is blue."

2
JUNE

I understand that life is complicated. In bad situations, I find the best possible solution, understanding that it doesn't need to be perfect.

3

Meditation:
BREATHE LIFE INTO FIRE

Sit or lie down in a comfortable position in which you can breathe easily. Keep your back straight and your eyes open or closed. Breathe in and out through your nose, extending your belly button on each inhale like you just had a large meal. Relax on the exhale.

See yourself sitting next to a campfire in the woods. Feel the heat from the flames and smell the smoke as it drifts over you. Reach down and touch the soil underneath you. With every exhale, visualize yourself blowing on the base of the fire, feeding it oxygen, making it bigger with every breath.

When thoughts enter your mind, see them appearing in the palm of your hand in the form of sticks. Label each one with a single word like "work" or "school" and then throw it into the fire. Watch it burn and turn into smoke.

Repeat for 5 to 10 minutes.

4
JUNE

Meditation:
MINDFUL WINDOW

Stand or sit in front of a window with your knees slightly bent, and your hands hanging toward the floor. As objects, people, and animals come into your vision, try not to name them or assign value judgments to them. Instead, focus on the colors, textures, and sounds that come from the images in the window.

Repeat for 5 to 10 minutes.

5
JUNE

How many blankets do you have on your bed? Where did they come from? Do they do a good job of keeping you warm?

6
JUNE

Two monks were arguing about a flag. The first monk said, "The flag is moving." The second monk said, "No, the wind is moving." Eventually, their teacher walked past and said, "Stop arguing about flags and finish your work in the garden."

7
JUNE

I am strong and capable. My knowledge and abilities help me find success in challenging moments.

8
JUNE

Meditation:
THE FIRE IN YOUR BELLY

Sit or lie down in a comfortable position in which you can breathe easily. Keep your back straight and your eyes open or closed. Breathe in and out through your nose, extending your belly button on each inhale like you just had a large meal. Relax on the exhale.

Visualize a campfire burning in the space behind your belly button. Notice the hot coals at the bottom of it and feel the heat from its flames. With every inhale, draw that heat into your torso, your arms, and your head. With every exhale, direct that energy into your legs and your feet.

Repeat for 5 to 10 minutes.

9

Meditation:

TAPPING UNDER THE EYES AND NOSE

Sit or lie down in a comfortable position in which you can breathe easily. Keep your back straight and your eyes open or closed. Breathe in and out through your nose, extending your belly button on each inhale like you just had a large meal. Relax on the exhale.

With the index and middle fingers of your right hand, tap the bone beneath your right eye eight times at a moderate pace. Then tap the bone between your nose and upper lip eight times. Finally, tap the bone beneath your left eye eight times. When you are finished, begin the process again.

Repeat for 5 to 10 minutes.

10
JUNE

Think about a time when you were happy. How did that feel in your body? Were your shoulders tight or relaxed? Were your hands in tight fists or relaxed at your side?

11
JUNE

A student sat down in front of their teacher and said, "I've finished all of my work for the day and now I'm ready to practice Zen." The teacher replied, "Good, you can start by helping other people with their work."

12
JUNE

—

Meditation:
LOVING YOURSELF

Stand or sit in front of a mirror. Keep your back straight and let your hands hang limply toward the floor. Breathe in and out through your nose, extending your belly button on each inhale like you had a large meal. Relax on the exhale.

Look at yourself in the mirror. Take a moment to connect with the current version of you. Remember your likes, dislikes, and dreams for the future.

Smile at yourself gently and repeat these words aloud: "May you be happy. May you be healthy. May you be safe. May you be loved." Keep repeating the mantra slowly and gently.

Repeat for 5 to 10 minutes.

13
JUNE

—

*My knowledge of the world and how it works
is constantly growing. I learn from everyone
I meet and get smarter every moment.*

14
JUNE

—

Meditation:
MINDFUL TEA DRINKING

Sit at a table with a hot cup of tea and offer gratutude to it. Think about the different elements of the tea that come together to make this drink possible.

Offer gratitude to all that made this cup of tea possible. Hold the cup in your hand and feel its warmth. Take a drink of tea and pause to notice any changes that happen in your body.

Repeat for 5 to 10 minutes.

15
JUNE

Write a letter to the version of yourself that will exist 10 years from now. Describe the things you are doing to make that version of you a success.

16
JUNE

A Zen teacher couldn't sleep because there was a monster making noise under their bed. The teacher went to the kitchen and grabbed a cookie, which they threw under the bed. The monster ate the cookie and went to sleep. The teacher went to sleep soon after.

17
JUNE

I don't believe in scarcity. I'm confident that as long as I treat people well, my needs will be met.

18
JUNE

Meditation:
MINDFUL MOON GAZING

Look up at the moon. Offer it gratitude for providing light on dark nights. Notice its shape. Is it a crescent, a half circle, or a full circle? Think about all the people throughout history who have stared up at the moon just like you're doing right now. Recognize that this experience connects you with every person who has ever looked up at the night sky.

Repeat for 5 to 10 minutes.

19
JUNE
—

Write a letter to the version of yourself that will exist five years from now. Describe the things you are doing that will make life harder for them. Can these things be changed?

20
JUNE
—

A student sat down in front of their teacher and asked, "What should I do if my legs start to hurt during seated meditation?" The teacher replied, "Switch to standing meditation."

21
JUNE
—

I set clear boundaries around how I want to be treated. And I don't hesitate to tell people when those boundaries have been violated.

22
JUNE
—

Meditation:
MINDFUL SITTING

Sit down in a chair. Take a few breaths and notice the physical sensations of sitting. Are your feet flat against the floor? Is your back leaning against the chair? How does the seat of the chair feel against your legs? Shift your position slightly and notice what changes.

Repeat for 5 to 10 minutes.

23
JUNE

Write a letter to yourself from the perspective of your parents or caregivers. In the letter, say all of the things that you wish they would say to you.

24
JUNE

A student asked their teacher, "What is the purpose of life?" The teacher asked, "What are you doing right now?" The student said, "I'm sitting on a cushion." The teacher replied, "The purpose of life is to sit on a cushion." The student said, "Later, I will pick up my kids from school." The teacher replied, "Later, the purpose of life will be to pick up your kids from school."

25
JUNE

Do you have a pet? Write a letter to your companion animal, detailing how you feel about them and why. If you don't have a pet, write a letter to a wild animal that you like.

26
JUNE

A student sat down in front of their teacher and asked, "How can I save all sentient beings from suffering?" The teacher replied, "Start by saving just one."

27
JUNE

Who is the person you trust more than anyone in the world? Describe in writing five things they've done over the years to earn your trust.

28
JUNE

A student sat down in front of their teacher and asked, "How do we practice the Buddha Dharma?" The teacher replied, "When people are hungry, feed them. When people are tired, give them a place to rest."

29
JUNE

What are five things you need from people in order to feel safe around them? Write about why these things are important to you and how you can communicate your needs to others.

30
JUNE

A Buddhist teacher was walking to the meditation hall when they noticed a pile of dirty dishes. The teacher took the dishes to the kitchen sink, cleaned them, put them away, and then went to the meditation hall. When the teacher got to the hall the students asked, "Why are you late for Dharma practice?" The teacher replied, "I already did Dharma practice," and walked out.

JULY

1
JULY

A bird flew from one cloud to the next in search of the sky. A student sat on the cushion in search of inner peace. Each of them looked for things that didn't need to be found.

2
JULY

I know that timing is everything. I am patient when it's time to wait for the right opportunity, and I don't hesitate to take advantage when the right one comes my way.

3
JULY

Meditation:
BOILING WATER

Sit or lie down in a comfortable position in which you can breathe easily. Keep your back straight and your eyes open or closed. Breathe in and out through your nose, extending your belly button on each inhale like you just had a large meal. Relax on the exhale.

Visualize yourself sitting next to a fireplace. Feel the heat from the flames and smell the smoke as it drifts over you. Reach down and touch the floor underneath you. With every exhale, notice that the flames get bigger and emit more heat. With every inhale, they get smaller.

Notice a large pot filled with water hanging over the fire. Using your fire breath, send heat into the pot and bring the water to a boil. As the pot heats up, notice the bubbles forming on the bottom of it. When the water starts to boil, listen to the bubbles pop, and watch the steam rise from its surface.

Repeat for 5 to 10 minutes.

4

Meditation:
MINDFUL HANDS

Sit or lie down in a comfortable position. Your eyes can be closed or pointed down toward the floor at a 45-degree angle. Bend your arms so that your forearms are parallel with the floor and rotate your palms up so they are facing the sky.

Inhale and exhale through your nose. On the exhale, touch the tip of your thumb to your index finger. Inhale and exhale again. On the exhale touch the tip of your thumb to your middle finger. Continue in this way until your thumb is touching the tip of your pinky finger, then restart the pattern by touching your thumb to the tip of your index finger.

Repeat for 5 to 10 minutes.

5
JULY

Turn off all your devices for an hour and engage in an activity that doesn't involve screens or electronics. Write about how you felt during the experience and what you notice about your mind-state.

6
JULY

A student sat down in front of their teacher and asked, "How do caterpillars turn into butterflies?" The teacher replied, "Caterpillars don't become butterflies. Butterflies become butterflies."

7
JULY

I trust my inner wisdom. If I'm not able to get all of the necessary information to make a decision, I know my intuition will guide me.

8
JULY

I understand that both my body and my mind need rest to function properly. I take time out each day to recharge without feelings of guilt or shame.

9
JULY

Meditation:
SHIRT ON SKIN

Sit or lie down in a comfortable position in which you can breathe easily. Keep your back straight and your eyes open or closed. Breathe in and out through your nose, extending your belly button on each inhale like you just had a large meal. Relax on the exhale.

Notice the physical sensation of your shirt against your skin. Is it soft? Is it scratchy? Where is it tight against your body and where is it loose? Notice the physical sensations without judgment and then move slightly, perhaps leaning forward or lifting your left shoulder.

How did the feeling of your shirt against your skin change? How did it remain the same? Keep moving, experimenting with different positions and noticing the feeling of your shirt rubbing against your body.

Repeat for 5 to 10 minutes.

10
JULY

Meditation:
MINDFUL EYES

Sit or lie down in a comfortable position in which you can breathe easily. Keep your back straight. Breathe in and out through your nose, extending your belly button on each inhale like you just had a large meal. Relax on the exhale. With each breath, alternate between having your eyes open and having them closed. One breath is equal to one full inhalation followed by one full exhalation.

If you don't want to close your eyes, alternate moving your head from left to right with each breath. Try to keep your gaze soft, not focusing on any objects.

Repeat for 5 to 10 minutes.

11
JULY

If you were a bird, how would you describe the experience of flying to a fish?

12
JULY

A student asked their teacher, "Why are dogs so happy?" The teacher replied, "When they are hungry, they eat. When they are tired, they sleep."

13
JULY

My powers of concentration are powerful, and they get better each day. When I'm working on a project, it gets my full attention.

14
JULY

Meditation:
TENDING THE THOUGHT CANDLE

Sit or lie down in a comfortable position in which you can breathe easily. Keep your back straight and your eyes open or closed. Breathe in and out through your nose, extending your belly button on each inhale like you just had a large meal. Relax on the exhale.

Visualize a candle sitting on the floor in front of you. The candle is unlit until a thought enters your mind. Thoughts cause the candle wick to catch fire. Focus on the physical sensations of your breathing and on the candle. If a thought causes the candle to catch fire, blow it out, and return your focus to your breathing.

Repeat for 5 to 10 minutes.

15
JULY

—

Meditation:
MINDFUL BREATHING

Sit or lie down in a comfortable position in which you can breathe easily. Keep your back straight and your eyes open or closed. Breathe in and out through your nose, extending your belly button on each inhale like you just had a large meal. Relax on the exhale. With your right hand, gently place your index finger and your thumb on either side of your nose. Breathe in and out five times with both nostrils open. Then take your thumb and press your right nostril closed. Breathe in and out five times and then alternate, using your index finger to close your left nostril while removing your thumb from your nose.

Breathe in and out five times, then begin the pattern again by removing your index finger from your nose and breathing in and out five times with both nostrils open.

Repeat for 5 to 10 minutes.

16
JULY

A young person approached their teacher after a Dharma talk and asked, "How do I find inner peace." The teacher replied, "The floor is dirty, go sweep it." The student said, "I don't want to sweep the floor, I want to find inner peace." The teacher sat in silence.

17
JULY

I trust my inner wisdom. If I'm not able to get all of the necessary information to make a decision, I know my intuition will guide me.

18
JULY

Meditation:
FLYING BIRDS

Sit or lie down in a comfortable position in which you can breathe easily. Keep your back straight and your eyes open or closed. Breathe in and out through your nose, extending your belly button on each inhale like you just had a large meal. Relax on the exhale.

Visualize yourself sitting in an open field with a clear blue sky above. There is a single black bird flying in the sky. Watch it fly as it dips and dives through the air. Each time a thought enters your head, label it as pleasant, unpleasant, or neutral, and picture another bird flying in the sky with the first one.

Don't try to stop your thoughts or get rid of the birds. Just enjoy watching them fly through the sky.

Repeat for 5 to 10 minutes.

19
JULY

Meditation:
MINDFUL FEET

Sit comfortably in a chair with your feet flat on the floor. Keep your back straight and your eyes open or closed. Breathe in and out through your nose, extending your belly button on each inhale like you just had a large meal. Relax on the exhale. Slowly begin lifting your left foot off the floor, the slower, the better. Notice the change in pressure in various parts of your foot. Did your toes begin to move first or did your heel move first?

See how high you can lift your foot while still having some part of it touching the floor. In the moment just before your foot breaks contact with the floor, slowly lower it back to the ground. Then go through the same process with your right foot.

Repeat for 5 to 10 minutes.

20
JULY

Write out five things that you enjoy about your job. Are there ways that you can do more of those things as part of your work?

21
JULY

A student sat down in front of their teacher and asked, "How do we practice the Way?" The teacher replied, "The whole world turns on a bowl of rice milk."

22
JULY

I choose my words carefully. I use my voice to bring happiness and contentment to the people around me.

23
JULY

Fill in the blank: I am happiest when I'm _____. Break the experience apart and write about specific qualities that make it enjoyable. Can you recreate some of those qualities in other areas of your life?

24
JULY

—

Meditation:
DODGING ICEBERGS

Sit or lie down in a comfortable position in which you can breathe easily. Keep your back straight and your eyes open or closed. Breathe in and out through your nose, extending your belly button on each inhale like you just had a large meal. Relax on the exhale.

Visualize yourself riding in a large boat on the open ocean. The sky is gray and a cold wind is blowing against your skin as the boat races through the water. Each time a thought enters your mind, label it "Thinking about _____." For example, if your dog enters your mind, you would label it "Thinking about dog."

For each thought that appears in your mind, visualize an iceberg appearing in the ocean. See the boat dodging the thought-iceberg by moving to either to the left or the right of it. Don't try to stop your thoughts or keep the icebergs from forming. Just dodge them with a sense of ease, and enjoy riding in the boat.

Repeat for 5 to 10 minutes.

25
JULY

Meditation:
MINDFUL MOANING

Sit or lie down in a comfortable position. Place your right hand over your heart and your left hand over your belly button. Inhale through the nose. Exhale out of your mouth and make whatever sound feels appropriate. Experiment with making different facial expressions. How does it feel to be louder? How does it feel to be quieter? Try making different facial expressions or holding your head at different angles as you make sounds.

Repeat for 5 to 10 minutes.

26
JULY

Write out five things that you dislike about your job. Are there ways that you can do less of those things at your work?

27
JULY

An old priest decided that it was time to retire. There was a large, crooked tree in front of his temple. He placed a sign in front of it that said, "I'll give my temple to anyone who can fix this tree." Many people came and offered suggestions, but he chased them away with a stick.

Finally, a young Zen student came to the temple, read the sign, looked at the tree, and bowed down to it three times. "Come inside," the priest said, "I have much to show you."

28
JULY

Meditation:
STANDING IN THE OCEAN

Sit or lie down in a comfortable position in which you can breathe easily. Keep your back straight and your eyes open or closed. Breathe in and out through your nose, extending your belly button on each inhale like you just had a large meal. Relax on the exhale.

Visualize yourself standing in the ocean with the water coming up to your chest. You can taste the salt in the air. The water temperature is cold and refreshing. Each time a thought enters your mind, label it as pleasant, unpleasant, or neutral. Then visualize a wave washing over your body, removing the thought from your mind.

Don't try to stop your thoughts or control the waves. Just enjoy resting in the ocean and feeling the water against your skin.

Repeat for 5 to 10 minutes.

29
JULY

A Buddhist teacher was working in their garden. The teacher's back was bent with age, and the hot sun made them sweat profusely. A student asked the teacher, "Do you enjoy working under the hot sun?" The teacher replied, "No. I prefer to sit in the shade."

The student asked the teacher, "If you prefer to sit in the shade, why do you work so hard in the garden." The teacher replied, "No one can live my life but me."

30
JULY

Meditation:
NOTICING OUR HANDS

Sit or lie down in a comfortable position in which you can breathe easily. Keep your back straight and your eyes open or closed. Breathe in and out through your nose, extending your belly button on each inhale like you just had a large meal. Relax on the exhale.

Place your left hand in your lap with your palm facing toward your face. Place your right hand on top of your left with your palm facing your face. Lift your thumbs and place the tips of your thumbs together so that your hands form a tiny oval with your thumbs on top and your fingers on the bottom.

Focus your attention on your hands. Without judgment, notice the feelings of pressure and any tension that arises in your hands. If your mind wanders, bring your attention back to the physical sensations in your hands.

Repeat for 5 to 10 minutes.

If you had one year to become an expert at something you enjoy, what would it be? What's stopping you from becoming an expert in that thing?

AUGUST

1

A student sat down in front of their teacher and said, "My enemy keeps sending me emails, I get mad every time I read them." The teacher replied, "If the emails make you mad, why do you keep reading them?"

2

I seek out people who have more wisdom than me. I use the information I gain from them to lead a happier, more content life.

3

Meditation:
FINGERTIPS ON SCALP

Sit or lie down in a comfortable position in which you can breathe easily. Keep your back straight and your eyes open or closed. Breathe in and out through your nose, extending your belly button on each inhale like you just had a large meal. Relax on the exhale.

Spread the fingers on both hands as wide as you can. Notice the amount of empty space between each finger. Place your fingertips on your scalp. Gently rub your scalp with your fingertips and notice the sensations that arise.

Is your hair coarse or silky? Can you tell where your fingertips end and your scalp begins? When thoughts arise in your mind, bring your focus back to the physical sensations in your fingertips and your scalp.

Repeat for 5 to 10 minutes.

4

Meditation:
MINDFUL WRITING

Sit down in a comfortable position with a pen and something to write on. Place the pen on the paper and focus on the physical sensations of breathing. When thoughts enter your mind, write them on the paper using the following format, "Thinking about _____." Don't try to justify or understand the thoughts. Just annotate them and return to focusing on your breath.

Repeat for 5 to 10 minutes.

5
AUGUST

Write about a time when you were so angry that you did something you regretted. Write about the experience, paying special attention to the physical sensations you felt.

6
AUGUST
—

A student sat down in front of their teacher and asked, "What is the core of spiritual practice?" The teacher replied, "It's like wiping dust from a mirror."

7
AUGUST
—

I am not afraid of conflict. I know my point of view is valid and I don't hesitate to stand up for myself.

8
AUGUST

—

Meditation:
LOVING-KINDNESS WITH A PARTNER

Sit or lie down in a comfortable position in which you can breathe easily. Keep your back straight and your eyes open or closed. Breathe in and out through your nose, extending your belly button on each inhale like you just had a large meal. Relax on the exhale.

Sit across from your partner (they can be a friend, sibling, parent, etc.) and stare into their eyes. Smile gently at each other and take turns reciting this mantra: "May you be happy. May you be healthy. May you be safe. May you be loved."

If you don't have a partner, recite the mantra to yourself in the mirror.

Repeat for 5 to 10 minutes.

9
AUGUST

Meditation:
MINDFUL ARM RAISES

Stand or sit with your feet shoulder-width apart and your knees slightly bent. Keep your back straight and your eyes open or closed. Breathe in and out through your nose, extending your belly button on each inhale like you just had a large meal. Relax on the exhale. As you start to fall into a rhythm with your breath, raise your arms in front of you on every inhale, and lower them to your sides on every exhale.

Repeat for 5 to 10 minutes.

10
AUGUST

Write five things that you are grateful for in your life. Who are the people who make those things possible?

11
AUGUST

A Buddhist teacher was playing fetch in the park with their dog. Every time the teacher threw the ball, the dog would find it and bring it back to the teacher. Eventually, the teacher stopped throwing the ball, so the dog laid down and went to sleep.

12
AUGUST

I am an expert at learning new things. I get excited each time I'm presented with new information, and I use it to improve the world around me.

13
AUGUST

—

Meditation:
FISH IN A CAVE

Sit or lie down in a comfortable position in which you can breathe easily. Keep your back straight and your eyes open or closed. Breathe in and out through your nose, extending your belly button on each inhale like you just had a large meal. Relax on the exhale.

Visualize yourself sitting at the bottom of a lake. The silt on the lake floor is cold and gritty against your legs. The water temperature is cold and refreshing. In front of you is a dark cave. You can't see inside, but you can tell it is very deep.

Each time a thought enters your mind, visualize an orange fish coming out of the cave. As it swims around, label the fish-thought pleasant, unpleasant, or neutral, and then watch it swim back into the cave. Don't try to control your thoughts or stop the fish from appearing. Just label each one and wish it well as it goes back into the cave.

Repeat for 5 to 10 minutes.

14

—

Meditation:
MINDFUL PAPER ON THE WALL

Tear a piece of notebook paper into four roughly square pieces. With the thumb and index fingers of each hand, hold the paper against the wall. Fill your lungs with as much air as you can and then blow onto the paper with your mouth.

As you are blowing on the paper, remove your fingers from it and try to keep the paper on the wall with just your breath. If you're unsuccessful, try tearing the paper into smaller pieces.

Repeat for 5 to 10 minutes.

15
AUGUST

—

How many pairs of shoes do you have in your closet? Write about what your life would be like if you didn't have shoes to wear.

16
AUGUST

—

A cat was hungry, so it went to its food bowl and ate. Then it needed to make a bowel movement, so it went to the litter box and made a deposit. Finally, the cat was tired, so it jumped up in the window and took a nap.

17
AUGUST

—

I understand that helping other people is a simple, effective way to help myself.

18
AUGUST

—

Meditation:
MINDFUL SMILE

Stand in front of the mirror and strike a pose as if you were a model in a magazine. Say aloud one good thing you like about either your personality or your appearance, then smile flirtatiously at yourself. Say, "Thanks for the compliment," and strike another pose.

Repeat for 5 to 10 minutes.

19
AUGUST

—

Is there food in your refrigerator? Write about the people who make it possible for that food to be there. Would your life be better or worse without their efforts?

20
AUGUST
—

A farmer went into a chicken coop and put out fresh water for the birds. The chickens ran toward the fresh water, but on the way, they saw a mud puddle filled with dirty water. The chickens drank from the mud puddle, and the fresh water remained untouched.

21
AUGUST
—

I understand that my choices have consequences. I weigh my options carefully to make the right decision.

22
AUGUST

—

Meditation:
MINDFUL BELL RINGING

Sit or lie down in a comfortable position. Find an object or a video that can make noise. Try to hear the exact moment when the sound starts and the exact moment when the sound stops. Experiment with making the noise loudly and softly.
   Repeat for 5 to 10 minutes.

23
AUGUST

—

How much time do you spend on social media every day? Write about the feelings you have during this time and whether social media makes you happy.

24
AUGUST

A fly was buzzing around in the air when a frog ate it. The frog was resting on a lily pad when a fish ate it. The fish was swimming in the river when it was caught by a fisherman. The fisherman ate the fish while a fly buzzed around his head.

25
AUGUST

Write down the things you do to keep your pet comfortable and safe, and how they repay this. If you don't have pets, watch a video of animals and write down how they interact with their owners or other animals.

26

AUGUST

———

A bird flew through a cloud in the sky. Both the bird and cloud were unharmed. A child watched the bird fly through the cloud and got an idea. They picked up a baseball and threw it at a window. The window shattered into a million pieces.

27
AUGUST
—

Imagine you got to spend a day as a cloud. Would you be a rain cloud or a white, fluffy cloud? What would your day be like? What are some of the things you would see?

28
AUGUST
—

A fish swam through the ocean, searching for water. A student walked into a meditation hall, searching for inner peace.

29
AUGUST

—

Write about what your life would be like if you stopped trying to impress other people.

30
AUGUST

—

A student sat down in front of their teacher and asked, "Why do sea turtles go back to the place they were born to lay their eggs?" The teacher replied, "We all must return to the source."

31
AUGUST

—

Meditation:
ROOTED LIKE A TREE

Sit comfortably in a chair with your feet flat on the ground. Keep your back straight and your eyes open or closed. Breathe in and out through your nose, extending your belly button on each inhale like you just had a large meal. Relax on the exhale.

Visualize your skin hardening and becoming coarse like wood. See your hair transforming into green leaves. With every inhale, bring air into your lungs. With every exhale, visualize roots sprouting from your feet and going deep into the earth. When thoughts enter your mind, imagine them as wind moving through your branches. They can't hurt you because your roots run deep.

Repeat for 5 to 10 minutes.

SEPTEMBER

1

SEPTEMBER

———

A worm lived its whole life in darkness. One day it poked its head up above the surface of the soil and saw the sun. The worm tried to tell its friends about the sun, but they didn't understand.

2

SEPTEMBER

———

Waiting is a game I love to play. I use downtime to learn new things that will help me in my journey.

3

Meditation:
ROCKS IN THE LAKE

Sit or lie down in a comfortable position in which you can breathe easily. Keep your back straight and your eyes open or closed. Breathe in and out through your nose, extending your belly button on each inhale like you just had a large meal. Relax on the exhale.

Visualize yourself standing on the shore of a lake. The water is perfectly still and you can see the forest and a blue sky being reflected in the water. Every now and then, a slight breeze causes the trees to rustle and the wind is warm against your skin.

There is a pile of round, black rocks next to you. Each time a thought enters your head, pick up a rock and label it with the thought. For example, if work entered your mind, label the rock "work." After you label the rock, throw it into the lake and watch the splash it makes as it hits the water.

Don't try to stop the thoughts or make the rocks go away. Just keep labeling rocks with your thoughts and throwing them into the water.

Repeat for 5 to 10 minutes.

4

Meditation:
MINDFUL ARM SQUEEZES

In a comfortable position with your back straight, breathe deeply. Place your right hand just above your left wrist. Give your left arm a firm squeeze and hold it as you count slowly to five. Focus on the physical sensation of your fingertips digging into your skin. Notice the amounts of pressure you feel in different parts of your hand. At the count of five, release your grip and move your hand higher up your arm. When you get to your shoulder, repeat the process with your left hand on your right arm.

Repeat for 5 to 10 minutes.

5
SEPTEMBER

What are five things that you try to keep people from knowing about you? What would happen if they found out?

6
SEPTEMBER

——

A gardener bought a houseplant and placed it in a window where it would get lots of sunlight. But the gardener forgot to water the plant, and it died.

7
SEPTEMBER

——

I'm not afraid to devote my entire self to the things I enjoy. I've earned the right to enjoy hobbies and spend time with loved ones.

8
SEPTEMBER

Meditation:
MINDFUL DRINK OF WATER

Fill a clear glass with water. Look at the water through the glass. Are there particles floating in it? Is it clear or does it have a tinge of color? Hold the glass in your hand and feel the temperature. Is it hot, lukewarm, or cold? Raise the glass to your lips, sip some water, and hold it in your mouth. What does it taste like? How does it feel against your tongue? Finally, swallow the water and notice the physical sensations.

Repeat for 5 to 10 minutes.

9
SEPTEMBER

What are five accomplishments that you are most proud of? What did it take for you to achieve them?

10
SEPTEMBER

A student sat down in front of their teacher and asked, "Why do dogs chase their tails?" The teacher replied, "Woof."

11
SEPTEMBER

I can focus my attention like a laser beam. When I'm working on a project, I'm not affected by distractions.

12
SEPTEMBER
———

Meditation:
WIGGLING TOES

Sit or lie down in a comfortable position in which you can breathe easily. Keep your back straight and your eyes open or closed. Breathe in and out through your nose, extending your belly button on each inhale like you just had a large meal. Relax on the exhale.

Wiggle your toes vigorously for several seconds. Dig them into the floor and rub them against your socks and shoes. Notice what that feels like, then stop. Each time a thought enters your mind, wiggle your toes and put your focus on the physical sensations that come from them.

Don't try to stop your thoughts, just wiggle your toes each time they arise. Repeat for 5 to 10 minutes.

13
SEPTEMBER

—

Meditation:
MINDFUL COMFORT OBJECT

Pick up an object in your home that conjures positive memories. Take a moment to think about your history with this object. How long have you had it? How did it come into your life? Hold it up to your nose and smell it. Rub it against your face and notice the texture. Close your left eye and look at the object closely; try to notice any interesting colors, shades, or patterns.

Repeat for 5 to 10 minutes.

14
SEPTEMBER

—

Write a love letter to your body, noting some of its best features and thanking it for carrying you through life.

15
SEPTEMBER

Two mice were walking down the hallway when they saw a mousetrap with cheese in it. The first mouse noticed the trap before noticing the cheese. The second mouse noticed the cheese before noticing the trap. Only one of them survived.

16
SEPTEMBER

I trust in the wisdom of nature. I take time each week to walk in the grass and sit under the trees.

17

Meditation:
CUTTING DOWN WEEDS

Sit or lie down in a comfortable position in which you can breathe easily. Keep your back straight and your eyes open or closed. Breathe in and out through your nose, extending your belly button on each inhale like you just had a large meal. Relax on the exhale.

Visualize yourself pushing a lawn mower in tall grass. Feel the handle underneath your fingers and the vibrations from the mower. The sun is shining and it's a beautiful day.

Each time a thought enters your mind, see red and green weeds pop up in front of the lawn mower. Label the weeds with your thoughts. For example, they might be "homework" or "grocery list," then cut them down with the mower.

Don't try to stop your thoughts or keep the weeds from growing. Just keep mowing them down.

Repeat for 5 to 10 minutes.

18
SEPTEMBER

Meditation:
MINDFUL HEARING

Sit or lie down comfortably. Close your eyes. If you don't want to close your eyes, limit visual distractions. Observe the sounds in your environment. Choose one sound to focus on.

Try to hear the sound without naming it or determining its location. Experience the sound with no thoughts or judgments.

Repeat for 5 to 10 minutes.

19
SEPTEMBER

What are some missed opportunities that came up over the last year that you wish you'd capitalized on? How can you make sure you're ready when they pop back up in the future?

20
SEPTEMBER

When a leaf falls to the ground, it shows every side of itself.
Accepting its fate, the leaf has nothing to hide.

21
SEPTEMBER

---

*My inner strength is boundless. My mindfulness
practice grants me deep spiritual reserves
that I can call upon at any moment.*

22

Meditation:
ENERGY ORB

Sit or lie down in a comfortable position in which you can breathe easily. Keep your back straight and your eyes open or closed. Breathe in and out through your nose, extending your belly button on each inhale like you just had a large meal. Relax on the exhale.

Place your palms on either side of your belly button, and use your breath to send energy into your hands. With every inhale, fill your lungs. With every exhale, visualize energy running from the center of your chest, down your arms, and into your hands.

As you continue to breathe, see the energy begin to form a ball between the palms of your hands. The energy ball is your favorite color. Move your hands and feel the shape of it. See if you can move it up and down.

Repeat for 5 to 10 minutes.

23
SEPTEMBER
—

Meditation:
MINDFUL MOVIE WATCHING

Begin watching a movie that you enjoy. Turn down the sound so you can see the action but you can't hear anything. Try to watch the movie without labeling anything (e.g., naming the characters or various objects in the scenes). Instead, try to focus on the colors, textures, and lighting that can be seen from one moment to the next.

Continue for 5 to 10 minutes.

24
SEPTEMBER
—

Write about your most valuable possession. What is its history and what makes it so special?

25
SEPTEMBER
—

A worm lived its whole life in darkness. One day it poked its head up above the surface of the soil and saw the sun. After it saw the sun, a bird swooped down and ate the worm. The worm had no regrets.

26
SEPTEMBER
—

Write a letter to the people who will live in your home after you. What are some stories you feel they should know?

27

Meditation:
HANDS ON BELLY

Sit or lie down in a comfortable position in which you can breathe easily. Keep your back straight and your eyes open or closed. Breathe in and out through your nose, extending your belly button on each inhale like you just had a large meal. Relax on the exhale.

Place your right hand over your belly button and your left hand over your heart. Breathe in and out five times, focusing on the feeling of your belly expanding and contracting under your hand. After five breaths, switch hands and breathe for another five breaths.

Repeat for 5 to 10 minutes.

28
SEPTEMBER
———

If you didn't have to eat, sleep, or use the bathroom, how would you spend your time?

29
SEPTEMBER
———

A chicken was scratching in the dirt, looking for worms to eat. A farmer came and gave the chicken some food and water. The chicken ate the food, drank the water, then went back to scratching in the dirt, looking for worms to eat.

30

SEPTEMBER

Meditation:

CLAPPING HANDS

Sit or lie down in a comfortable position in which you can breathe easily. Keep your back straight and your eyes open or closed. Breathe in and out through your nose, extending your belly button on each inhale like you just had a large meal. Relax on the exhale.

Hold your hands at chest level, about 12 inches apart. Every time a thought enters your mind, imagine it as a snowflake floating between your hands, and clap your hands together. Notice that when you take your hands apart, the thought has disappeared.

Repeat for 5 to 10 minutes.

OCTOBER

1
OCTOBER

A student was working in the garden. The teacher appeared and asked, "Manure makes our garden grow. What do evil thoughts do?" The student responded by continuing to work in the garden. The teacher smiled and walked away.

2
OCTOBER

I am confident in my skills and abilities. I have what I need to accomplish my personal and professional goals.

3

Meditation:

ROCKET SHIPS AND THE SUN

Sit or lie down in a comfortable position in which you can breathe easily. Keep your back straight and your eyes open or closed. Breathe in and out through your nose, extending your belly button on each inhale like you just had a large meal. Relax on the exhale.

Visualize yourself floating through outer space. There are stars twinkling in the distance all around you. Directly in front of you is a large, yellow sun that burns and pulses like living fire. When you drift closer to the sun, the front of your body gets warmer. When you drift farther away, the front of your body gets cooler.

Each time a thought enters your brain, label it as either pleasant, unpleasant, or neutral and visualize it turning into a tiny rocket ship. Send the rocket ship into the sun and watch it burst into flames.

Repeat for 5 to 10 minutes.

4

Meditation:
MINDFUL JUICE DRINKING

Pour yourself a glass of juice. Look at it closely and notice the color. What does it remind you of? Swish the juice around in the glass and look at the film it leaves behind. Is it thick or thin? Hold the juice up to your nose and take a whiff. Does the smell jog any memories? Take a sip and hold the juice on your tongue for several seconds before swallowing. What is the flavor sensation? Think back to the first time you had this beverage.

Repeat for 5 to 10 minutes.

5
OCTOBER

Who is the most courageous person you know? Think of times when they have shown great courage. How did this example affect you?

6
OCTOBER

Two students were coloring in coloring books. One was careful to stay within the lines. The other scribbled all over the page. Later that day, each student took a picture out of their coloring book and gave it to their teacher as a gift. The teacher responded with gratitude and put both pictures on the refrigerator.

7
OCTOBER

I have the knowledge I need to overcome any obstacle I encounter. If something is outside of my skill set, I'm not afraid to ask for help.

8

Meditation:
TAPPING YOUR CHEST

Sit or lie down in a comfortable position in which you can breathe easily. Keep your back straight and your eyes open or closed. Breathe in and out through your nose, extending your belly button on each inhale like you just had a large meal. Relax on the exhale.

Place your right hand over your heart and your left hand over your belly button. Bring your attention to your breath. Try to find the space between the moment your exhale is finished and the moment you start to inhale your next breath. During that space between breaths, tap your chest with the fingertips of your right hand twice before you inhale.

Repeat for 5 to 10 minutes.

9

Meditation:
MINDFUL VEGETABLE CUTTING

Grab your favorite vegetable and place it on a cutting board. If you don't have access to a vegetable, grab your favorite fruit. Offer it gratitude for the nourishment that it's about to provide you. Take a sharp knife and place it lightly on top of the vegetable without cutting it.

Ensure that your fingers are far away from the blade and begin to slowly apply downward pressure on the knife. Use your sense of touch to recognize the exact moment when the knife starts to cut the vegetable. At that moment, say, "Cut!"

If your chosen vegetable is safe to eat raw, take the piece you just cut off and place it on your tongue. Take a moment to notice its weight and texture in your mouth before you eat it.

Repeat for 5 to 10 minutes.

10
OCTOBER

—

**What does authenticity mean to you?
What are some things that are stopping
you from living an authentic life?**

11
OCTOBER

—

A student sat down in front of their teacher and said, "Everything is a mess. What should I do?" The teacher replied, "A single match can light many candles."

12
OCTOBER

I am generous with both my money and my attention.
The more I give, the more I have to give.

13
OCTOBER

Meditation:
MINDFUL HUG WITH A PARTNER

Enfold your partner in a hug. Using your sense of smell, notice any cologne, perfume, or hair products emanating from them. Using your sense of touch, notice the sensation of their clothing beneath your fingertips. Using your sense of hearing, notice if you can hear their breathing or their heartbeat. Using your sense of sight, notice what the world around you looks like from this position.

If you don't have a partner available, do the practice with a pillow. You can also wrap your arms around your torso and give yourself a hug.

Repeat for 5 or 10 minutes.

14

Meditation:
MINDFUL LEAF-RAKING

Stand or sit over the leaves with your feet shoulder-width apart. Hold the rake so that it's parallel to the ground with your palms facing the sky. Notice the weight of it in your hands. Notice the color and texture of the handle. Is it made from wood or plastic? Where did the rake come from?

Look over the area that you're about to rake. Have you spent a lot of time there over the past year? What are some of your favorite memories?

Begin raking the area slowly and methodically. Listen to the sound the rake makes as it contacts leaves. Are the leaves dry and crispy or wet and slimy?

Repeat for 5 to 10 minutes.

15
OCTOBER

When you hear the phrase "a person of good character," what comes to mind? What are some techniques you use to deal with people of poor character?

16
OCTOBER

A monk was walking in the garden with the abbot of their temple. When they stopped for a break, the monk asked, "How can we live a peaceful life?" The abbot replied, "Start by living a peaceful day."

17
OCTOBER

I keep my word. People respect me because they know I can be trusted to keep their secrets and work for their best interests.

18
OCTOBER

Meditation:
ALTERNATE CHEST AND BELLY TAPPING

Sit or lie down comfortably. Breathe in and out through your nose, extending your belly button on each inhale like you just had a large meal. Relax on the exhale.

Place your right hand over your heart and your left hand over your belly button. Bring your attention to your breath. With every inhale, tap your chest one time with your right hand. With every exhale, tap your belly button with your left hand.

Repeat for 5 or 10 minutes.

19
OCTOBER

Meditation:
MINDFUL TREE GAZING

Position yourself in front of a tree. Grab it with both hands, close your eyes, and notice the tree's texture with your fingertips. Are there other objects in your life that feel this way? Open your eyes and look at the tree's bark. Is it a single color or multiple colors? Lean in and give the tree a whiff. What food does a tree smell like? Put your ear against the tree's trunk. Are there any sounds emanating from it?

Repeat for 5 to 10 minutes.

20
OCTOBER

Are you a decisive person? If so, write about a time when your decisiveness got you into trouble. Could this have been avoided?

21
OCTOBER

A student asked their teacher, "How should we respond to inescapable suffering?" The teacher replied, "Stop trying to escape it."

22
OCTOBER

I don't make snap decisions. I weigh my options carefully and make choices that improve my life and the lives of others.

23

Meditation:
ALTERNATING HEAD MOVEMENTS

Sit or lie down in a comfortable position in which you can breathe easily. Keep your back straight and your eyes open or closed. Breathe in and out through your nose, extending your belly button on each inhale like you just had a large meal. Relax on the exhale.

Begin with your chin hanging over your right shoulder. Inhale and slowly move your head to center. Try to time it so your face is facing forward at the same time as you finish inhaling. Exhale and move your chin toward your left shoulder. Try to time it so your face is facing all the way left by the time you finish exhaling. Next, inhale and bring your head back to center.

Repeat for 5 to 10 minutes.

24
OCTOBER

Meditation:
MINDFUL FLOWER GAZING

Stand in front of a flower. Rub your fingers along its stem and blossom, noticing the different textures. Compare the sensations to furniture you have in your home. Look closely at the blossom. How many colors and shades of color can you see in it? Close your eyes and sniff the flower. Is it a strong aroma? What does it smell like?

Repeat for 5 to 10 minutes.

25
OCTOBER

Think of someone you know who is outgoing and engaging. How do you feel when you are around them?

26
OCTOBER

A candle doesn't worry about being big or small. It just burns with its entire being, bringing light into the world. We must live our lives as if we are candles.

27
OCTOBER

Pretend you are a version of yourself that exists five years in the future. Write a letter to the version of you that exists today, explaining what you've accomplished and how you overcame obstacles along the way.

Meditation:
TRACING YOUR FOREARM

Sit or lie down in a comfortable position in which you can breathe easily. Keep your back straight and your eyes open or closed. Breathe in and out through your nose, extending your belly button on each inhale like you just had a large meal. Relax on the exhale.

Bend your left arm at the elbow and rotate your hand so that your palm is facing toward your head. Place the first two fingers of your right hand on your left wrist.

Inhale and slowly move your fingers from your wrist toward the crook of your left arm, stopping once you either finish your inhale or reach the crook of your left arm. Exhale and move your fingers toward your wrist, stopping either when you finish exhaling or reach your wrist.

Repeat for 5 to 10 minutes.

29
OCTOBER

What scares you? Where did this fear come from, and what are some ways that you cope with it?

30
OCTOBER

A student sat down in front of their teacher and asked, "How should we treat people who are mean to us?" The teacher replied, "When you meet a porcupine, be kind. But don't give them a hug."

31

Meditation:
FINGER TAPPING

Sit or lie down on the floor in a comfortable position in which you can breathe easily. Keep your back straight and your eyes open or closed. Breathe in and out through your nose, extending your belly button on each inhale like you just had a large meal. Relax on the exhale.

Place your right hand on the floor so that your fingertips are lightly touching it. Inhale and tap your thumb on the floor eight times. Exhale and tap your index finger on the floor eight times. Inhale and tap your middle finger on the floor eight times. Continue in this way until you get to your little finger, then start back at your thumb. Experiment with tapping faster or slower.

Repeat for 5 to 10 minutes.

NOVEMBER

1
NOVEMBER
—

A student asked their teacher, "Why do I feel empty when I use social media?" The teacher replied, "A picture of food won't quell our hunger."

2
NOVEMBER
—

My energy is steady and ongoing. Each time I accomplish one of my goals, I feel encouraged to tackle the next one.

3
NOVEMBER

Meditation:
TEMPLE ROTATIONS

Sit or lie down in a comfortable position in which you can breathe easily. Keep your back straight and your eyes open or closed. Breathe in and out through your nose, extending your belly button on each inhale like you just had a large meal. Relax on the exhale.

Take the index finger on each hand and place them gently on your temples. With every inhale, rotate your fingers in circles on your temples. Stop the movement on every exhale.

Repeat for 5 to 10 minutes.

4
NOVEMBER

—

Meditation:
MINDFUL CANDLE

Light a candle. Take a whiff and notice if there are any smells coming from it. Look closely and see if there is any smoke emanating from the flame. Touch the candle holder and notice its texture. Finally, watch the candle flame flicker. If your mind wanders, just bring your focus back to the burning candle.

Repeat for 5 to 10 minutes.

5
NOVEMBER

—

List five people who helped you get where you are today. Brainstorm ways that you can follow their example and help other people the way they helped you.

6
NOVEMBER

A monk was walking with the abbot of their temple. When they stopped for a rest, the monk asked, "How do I forgive myself for mistakes I've made in the past?" The abbot replied, "Place your past mistakes on the ground in front of me, and I'll show you how to forgive them." The monk said, "I can't place my mistakes in front of you." The abbot replied, "Then they are already forgiven."

7
NOVEMBER

My ability to concentrate is superb. When I feel scattered, I focus on my breath to center myself.

8
NOVEMBER

Meditation:
EYES OPEN, EYES CLOSED

Sit or lie down comfortably. Keep your back straight. Breathe in and out through your nose, extending your belly button on each inhale like you just had a large meal. Relax on the exhale.

With your eyes open, take four slow, deep breaths. Close your eyes and take four more slow, deep breaths. Open your eyes and continue the pattern.

Repeat for 5 to 10 minutes.

9
NOVEMBER

Meditation:
MINDFUL RADIO LISTENING

While listening to music try not to attach any judgments or names. Just notice the highs and lows of the vibrations. Repeat for 5 to 10 minutes.

10
NOVEMBER
———

Write about something that happened in your life that you think could be inspirational to others.

11
NOVEMBER
———

A student sat down in front of their teacher and asked, "Why do cats poop in litter boxes?" The teacher replied, "Meow."

12
NOVEMBER

My inner wisdom is a gift that I offer to the world. I have everything I need inside of me to make good decisions.

13
NOVEMBER

A student sat down in front of their teacher and said, "I'm feeling discouraged. When I meditate, I feel good for a while, but then my mind becomes angry again. What should I do?" The teacher replied, "When you are hungry, eat. When you are tired, sleep."

14
NOVEMBER

Meditation:
BOX BREATHING

Sit or lie down in a comfortable position in which you can breathe easily. Keep your back straight and your eyes open or closed. Breathe in and out through your nose, extending your belly button on each inhale like you just had a large meal. Relax on the exhale.

Inhale and count to four. On the count of four, stop your inhale and hold your breath for four counts. On the count of four, stop holding your breath and exhale for four counts. On the count of four, stop your exhale and hold your breath for four counts.

Repeat for 5 to 10 minutes.

15
NOVEMBER

—

Meditation:
MINDFUL FINGERTIPS (ON CLOTHING)

Sit comfortably on the floor or in a chair. Send your awareness to your finger-tips. Reach down and touch the bottom of your feet. Are you wearing shoes or socks? What are the sensations you feel in your fingertips? Do the sensations change based on the colors, fabrics, or textures that your fingers touch? When you finish with your feet, continue slowly up your legs until you've touched all of your clothing.

Repeat for 5 to 10 minutes.

16
NOVEMBER

—

We all make mistakes. Write about a time that you did something you regret and discuss how you worked to make amends.

17
NOVEMBER
—

After a Dharma talk, a young person walked up to the teacher and said, "I'm so frustrated. The squirrels won't stop eating seeds from my bird feeder." The teacher responded by climbing a tree.

18
NOVEMBER
—

I take the feelings of other people into account without allowing myself to be bullied. When it's time to have difficult conversations, I am honest and forthright.

19
NOVEMBER

—

Meditation:
MINDFUL HEARTBEAT

Place the first two fingers of your right hand under the right side of your jaw. Move them around until you can feel your heartbeat. Count the beats of your heart up to 10, focusing on the physical sensation of your blood vessels pulsing beneath your fingertips. After you count 10 beats, start over again at one.

Repeat for 5 to 10 minutes.

20
NOVEMBER

—

Pretend you are writing a how-to book for your favorite hobby. What are the instructions or words of wisdom that you would give to a beginner?

21
NOVEMBER

A student sat down in front of their teacher and asked, "Why do we bow to the Buddha?" The teacher responded by standing up and bowing to the student.

22
NOVEMBER

I am spiritually and emotionally strong. I am resilient and I enjoy overcoming challenges.

23

Meditation:
MINDFUL BED MAKING

Strip the dirty sheets and blankets from the bed. Lie down on the bare mattress for a few moments and notice how it feels against your skin. What would it be like to sleep like that every night? Put fresh sheets on the bed. Rub your hands over them. What does the texture remind you of? Put your face close to the sheets and take a whiff. Is the smell unpleasant, pleasant, or neutral? Put fresh blankets on the bed and take note of their color. Try to remember where and when you got the blankets.

24
NOVEMBER

Write about a funny story that you were told recently. What happened? Where did it happen? How well do you know the people involved?

25
NOVEMBER

———

A merchant walked up to a Zen teacher and asked, "Is our mind defiled or is it pure?" The teacher replied by flipping a coin.

26
NOVEMBER

———

What was the greatest, most motivational event that you've ever witnessed? How has it impacted your life?

27
NOVEMBER

———

A student asked their teacher, "What should I do if I get too hot during meditation?" The teacher replied, "Turn on a fan."

28
NOVEMBER

———

Who is a friend or coworker you can always rely on when you need a dose of optimism in your life? Write about a time they helped you see the brighter side of things.

29
NOVEMBER
———

Two monks were sitting in the meditation hall. The first monk asked, "What's the point of practicing meditation if we're all going to die?" The second monk replied, "Practice now, die later."

30
NOVEMBER
———

We think a lot about the goals we want to accomplish, but what about the things we've already done? Write about where you were five years ago, and the obstacles you've overcome to get where you are today.

DECEMBER

1
DECEMBER

If you meet Buddha on the road, give him a hug.

2
DECEMBER

My knowledge of the world grows every day. I seek out books and teachers that help me become my best self.

3
DECEMBER

Meditation:
3–1 BREATHING

Sit or lie down in a comfortable position in which you can breathe easily. Keep your back straight and your eyes open or closed. Breathe in and out through your nose, extending your belly button on each inhale like you just had a large meal. Relax on the exhale.

Take three quick inhalations of air in a row and try to have your lungs full of air by the end of the third inhalation. Relax and empty your lungs with a single exhale.

Repeat for 5 to 10 minutes.

4
DECEMBER

Meditation:
MINDFUL LAUNDRY

Take a load of laundry out of the dryer. Take a moment to notice its warmth and smell. Dump the laundry out and separate it by colors. Which color do you wear the most? Pick three pieces of laundry and hold each one in your hands for one minute. Think back to when you got that piece of clothing, how long you've had it, and any fond memories associated with it.

Repeat for 5 to 10 minutes.

5
DECEMBER

Who are some of the most supportive people in your life? Write about some of the ways they've helped you over the years and times when you returned the favor.

6
DECEMBER

—

A student asked their teacher, "Why do snowballs melt in the sun?" The teacher replied, "Delusions disappear when they're met with truth."

7
DECEMBER

—

I am overwhelmed by the generosity of others. I've built a support system that assists me in my endeavors.

8

DECEMBER

Meditation:

ONE HAND OPEN, ONE HAND CLOSED

Sit or lie down in a comfortable position in which you can breathe easily. Keep your back straight and your eyes open or closed. Breathe in and out through your nose, extending your belly button on each inhale like you just had a large meal. Relax on the exhale.

Bend both of your arms at the elbow so that your forearms are perpendicular to your body. Rotate your hands so your palms face upward. Begin with your left hand open and your right hand closed in a loose fist. Inhale. At the end of the inhale, close your left hand and open your right hand. Exhale. At the end of the exhale, open your left hand and close your right hand.

Repeat for 5 to 10 minutes.

9
DECEMBER

Meditation:
MINDFUL STRETCHING

While sitting or standing, bend your knees slightly. Raise your arms above your head and slowly bend forward at the hips. Don't try to force yourself lower than what feels natural. Let your arms hang gently in front of you. Look around and notice what the room looks like from this angle. Send your focus to your hips and the backs of your legs. Notice any stretching or lengthening that is taking place.

Repeat for 5 to 10 minutes.

10
DECEMBER
—

Trust is integral to a good relationship. What are the criteria you use to determine if someone is trustworthy? What happens if they break that trust?

11
DECEMBER
—

It's easy to be kind to people if you see everyone as Buddha.

12
DECEMBER

—

I have a clear understanding of right and wrong. I investigate the motivations behind my actions to ensure they are rooted in compassion and wisdom.

13
DECEMBER

Meditation:
OPEN PALM TAPPING

Sit or lie down in a comfortable position in which you can breathe easily. Keep your back straight and your eyes open or closed. Breathe in and out through your nose, extending your belly button on each inhale like you just had a large meal. Relax on the exhale.

Open your left hand and rotate your palm so it faces upward. Use your right index finger to lightly tap the bottom of your left palm. Coordinate the tapping with your breath so that you tap eight times on every inhale and eight times on every exhale.

Repeat for 5 to 10 minutes.

14

Meditation:
MINDFUL SPLASHING

Stand at a sink and adjust the water temperature to lukewarm. Run your hands under the water and feel the physical sensations.

Cup the water in your hands and splash it on your face, massaging it. Focus on the physical sensations of the water and your hands against your face. Keep going until your face is mostly dry, then splash more water on.

Repeat for 5 to 10 minutes.

15
DECEMBER

How would you define the difference between knowledge and wisdom? Who is the most knowledgeable person you know? Who is the wisest?

16
DECEMBER
—

This world is an illusion. That doesn't stop it from being real.

17
DECEMBER
—

I have no problem waiting when that's what the moment demands. I use moments of inactivity to practice mindfulness.

18
DECEMBER

Two monks were sitting in the meditation hall. The first monk asked, "What happens to us when we find inner peace?" The second monk replied, "We're able to breathe again."

19
DECEMBER

Meditation:
HOLDING OUR SOCKS

Sit or lie down in a comfortable position in which you can breathe easily. Keep your back straight and your eyes open or closed. Breathe in and out through your nose, extending your belly button on each inhale like you just had a large meal. Relax on the exhale.

Grab two pairs of socks. Hold one pair in each hand. Inhale, and lift the socks in your right hand to just below shoulder level. Move the socks in your left hand to about waist level. Exhale, and lift the socks in your left hand to just below shoulder level. Move the socks in your right hand to about waist level. Continue alternating as you breathe. Notice the weight and sensation of the socks as they move.

Repeat for 5 to 10 minutes.

20
DECEMBER

Meditation:
MINDFUL LAUGHING

Sit down in a comfortable position. Think of a pleasant or comical memory and say, "Ha." Wait for a moment and then say, "Ha, ha." Continue in this way, adding one more "ha" each time. Be sure to notice the feeling of air in your throat and the contraction in your chest and stomach each time you make the "ha" sound.

Repeat for 5 to 10 minutes.

21
DECEMBER

What is the greatest lesson that you've learned from the natural world? How does it help you in daily life?

22
DECEMBER

—

After a Dharma talk, a candlemaker walked up to the teacher and asked, "Where does the flame go when you blow out a candle?" The teacher replied, "There is no candle."

23
DECEMBER

—

I never hesitate to get started when there's work to be done. I go after my goals vigorously and full of confidence.

24
DECEMBER

———

Meditation:
COLLARBONE TAPPING

Sit or lie down in a comfortable position in which you can breathe easily. Keep your back straight and your eyes open or closed. Breathe in and out through your nose, extending your belly button on each inhale like you just had a large meal. Relax on the exhale.

Place your right arm across your body, so that your right hand is resting lightly on your left collarbone. Begin gently tapping your collarbone and coordinate the tapping with your breath. Inhale and tap four times. Exhale and tap four times. Notice the physical sensations of tapping and experiment with tapping at different speeds.

Repeat for 5 to 10 minutes.

25
DECEMBER

—

Meditation:
MINDFUL WANTING

As you go through your day, narrate your actions with the phrase, "I want to _____." For example, if you are sitting on the couch, say, "I want to sit on the couch." If you are walking to the kitchen, say, "I want to walk to the kitchen." See what happens in your mind when you align your wants and desires to exactly what is happening in this moment.

Repeat for 5 to 10 minutes.

26
DECEMBER

—

What would your life be like if there was no electricity? How does it make your life better each day?

27
DECEMBER

—

Meditation:
FIELD OF DANDELIONS

Sit or lie down in a comfortable position in which you can breathe easily. Keep your back straight and your eyes open or closed. Breathe in and out through your nose, extending your belly button on each inhale like you just had a large meal. Relax on the exhale.

Visualize yourself standing in a field full of dandelions. Fluffy white clouds float through a blue sky, and the sun is warm against your skin. The dandelions are reaching the end of their lives, and their yellow petals have been replaced with white puff balls made from countless seeds.

Each time a thought enters your mind, label it, "Thinking about _____." Then pick one of the dandelions in the field and blow on the dandelion's seeds. As they float away, watch your thoughts float away with them.

Repeat for 5 to 10 minutes.

28
DECEMBER
———

What would your life be like if there was no indoor plumbing or running water? Who makes it possible for you to have these things?

29
DECEMBER
———

A student sat down in front of their teacher and asked, "Why do we need to practice meditation?" The teacher replied, "If a house doesn't have a roof, the rain gets in."

30
DECEMBER

Meditation:
PAINTING THE CANVAS

Sit or lie down in a comfortable position in which you can breathe easily. Keep your back straight and your eyes open or closed. Breathe in and out through your nose, extending your belly button on each inhale like you just had a large meal. Relax on the exhale.

Visualize yourself standing in front of a large, blank painter's canvas. There is a magic paint brush in your hand that paints whatever color you want without running dry. When a thought enters your mind, imagine it appearing as a single word on the canvas. For example, if you started thinking about a dog, the word *dog* would appear.

Every time a word appears on the canvas, paint over it with your magic brush. Don't try to control your thoughts; just keep breathing and painting over them.

Repeat for 5 to 10 minutes.

If you could be a star in a constellation, which constellation would you pick? What's special about that group of stars?

Resources

Visit my blog, *The Same Old Zen*, to read articles and view Dharma talks that connect spiritual practice with daily life: TheSameOldZen.com

If you enjoyed this book, check out my other one, *Perfectly Ordinary: Buddhist Teachings for Everyday Life*.

ABOUT THE AUTHOR

Alex Kakuyo is a Buddhist teacher and a breathwork facilitator. A former Marine, he served in both Iraq and Afghanistan before finding the Dharma through a series of happy accidents. Alex helps students connect Buddhist teachings with daily life through movement, mindfulness, and meditation. His books, Dharma talks, and other writings can be found at his blog, *The Same Old Zen*.